Foreword

This book is based on the research car[illegible]ut between 1987-1990 by members of the Derbyshire Archaeological Society as a project called the Derby Buildings Record. During the period they examined and recorded 72 buildings although not all of them were relevant to this study because some were not dwellings or were larger medieval houses. A list of those that were used is to be found at the end of the book.

I am most grateful to the many Archaeological Society members who have helped in this work. Additionally, Kenneth Boyce and Alwyn Davies have taken photographs to illustrate specific points, and I owe them particular thanks. I am also grateful to Maxwell Craven of Derby City Museum and Howard Usher of Melbourne Civic Society for their constant help and encouragement.

Above all, of course, I am indebted to the householders who have so kindly allowed us access and helped us in our work by their encouragement, often by showing us photographs taken during restoration or alterations, and sometimes by showing us deeds - not to mention many cups of coffee and practical help. I would like to emphasise that all the houses mentioned are private dwellings and not open to the public. It is important not to impose on the householders' kindness by any invasion of privacy.

Almost nothing has been written previously about the buildings in this area. An essay on Leicestershire buildings by Peter Eden in **Leicester and its Region** ed. N. Pye, Leicester University Press, 1972, makes some useful general observations. The **Derbyshire Archaeological Journal** includes descriptions of a few houses in some of its earlier volumes. For more about crucks, N. W. Alcock's **Cruck Construction: an Introduction and Catalogue** CBA 1981 is the standard reference, and a paper on Derbyshire crucks by F. Marston was published in **Derbyshire Archaeological Journal** 1967, pp 117-122.

The Derby Buildings Record continues its work of recording houses in the area around Derby, and will be glad to hear of other houses of historic interest.

Barbara Hutton, March 1991.

Derbyshire Archaeological Society Architectural Section

The DERBY BUILDINGS RECORD is part of the Architectural Section of the Derbyshire Archaeological Society, and is under the direction of Mrs Barbara Hutton, FSA. The purpose is to compile records of farmhouses, cottages and similar buildings in the area around Derby. These records consist of measured drawings and typed reports which are given to the householder, with copies deposited at the Derby City Museum, The Strand, Derby for research purposes. The DERBY BUILDINGS RECORD started in 1987 and recorded some 90 buildings in its first four years.

The porch of Hartshorne Manor as it was in 1979.
Photograph: Royal Commission on Historical Monuments England, Crown Copyright.

Historic Farmhouses Around Derby

BARBARA HUTTON

SCARTHIN BOOKS
1991

Contents

FOREWORD	Page (i)
EARLY VILLAGE HOUSES	5
HOUSE PLANS	6
Hearth Passage Houses	7
Lobby Entrance Houses	11
Direct Entry Plans	17
Double Pile Plans	21
STRUCTURE	23
Crucks	23
Roof Trusses	31
Wall Framing	36
Brick Walls	42
Stone Walls	47
INTERIOR FEATURES	48
Beams	48
Fireplaces	51
Stairs	51
Windows and Doors	53
Other Features	55
SUMMARY	57
INDEX AND GAZETTEER	58

Early Village Houses

In the villages around Derby the ordinary houses in the Middle Ages were built of timber. A timber frame was first erected and then the wall panels were filled with wattle and daub, producing an effect such as we can see in many of these villages today. This way of building, however, went on for a long time and the houses that now remain are not usually medieval but were built in the sixteenth or seventeenth centuries. After that, brick and in some places stone became the favoured building materials. In the late 18th century when the village fields were enclosed, new farmhouses were built outside the village centres on the land allocated to them by the Enclosure Awards. These houses are distinctive. Built of brick, often with slate roofs, they were usually three storeys tall and two rooms deep, often with an M-shaped roofline; they had central front doors with the windows arranged symmetrically on each side. It is with the houses built between these extremes - later than the Middle Ages but before the Enclosure Awards - that we are here chiefly concerned. They form the characteristic house types of this region during an important building period, and it is because so many remain that we can infer that the region was prosperous at the time they were built. On the other hand it must have been rather less prosperous later on, because in the village centres these houses were not demolished when the new farmhouses were built out in the fields, but were divided up and used as cottages. Houses in the village street are now in most cases purely residential, but you can often find some of their former farm buildings surviving behind them, showing that they were once farmsteads. In fact, nearly all village houses were once farms - manor houses were usually the base of a farming operation, and cottages often had a smallholding attached.

House plans

The design of these houses falls into one of several fairly clearly defined groups, designs which, one after the other, seem to have had fashionable phases and then to have declined in popularity. There are houses with hearth-passage entries, houses with lobby entries either against a central stack or against an end stack, and houses with their entrance directly into the chief livingroom. Then in the 18th century separate entrance-halls began to be built.

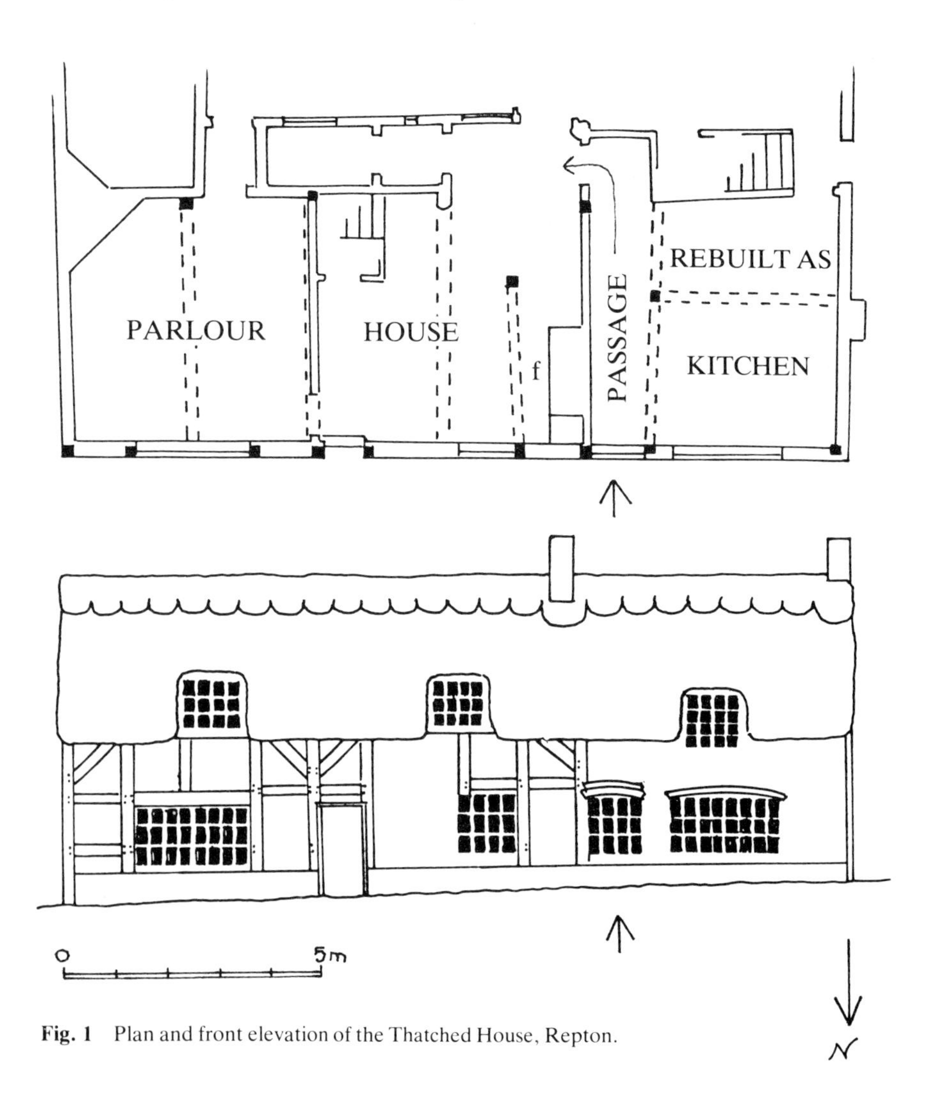

Fig. 1 Plan and front elevation of the Thatched House, Repton.

HEARTH-PASSAGE HOUSES.

We will begin by considering hearth-passage entries. In these houses the front door opens into a passage running through the house from front to back behind the main hearth, and the way into the houseplace (or living-room) is from that passage. A good example of this plan is the Thatched House opposite Repton Church *(Fig. 1)*. The original main entrance is now converted into a window; formerly it led into a passage, now marked out by a ceiling beam on the line of the partition that divided it from the room to the west. At the far end of the passage a door led east into the main livingroom, which formerly had an inglenook fireplace backing on to the passage - its hearth-beam can be seen in the ceiling. Beyond the livingroom to the east is the parlour, which in the seventeenth century was still normally the principal bedchamber but later took on the functions of the best sittingroom. A new front door has been made directly into the livingroom, but that does not obscure the original design, it simply shows that at some later date a new design became fashionable. A house exactly like this one, even to the precise dimensions, is found in Castle Square, Melbourne. To get to the front door you go through the garden gate to the north side of the house. A door opens into what was once a passage, with marks in the ceiling to show where the partition was on its west side. The passage crosses the house to a blocked doorway at the south end, but before that you turn east into the livingroom and see the reconstructed inglenook fireplace backing on to the passage. Beyond the houseplace to the east is what was originally the parlour, now turned into an entrance hall with a door from the garden. Both houses, of course, have later been extended.

Two other houses in Melbourne follow this general design. One is the well-known cruck house in the High Street *(Fig. 20)*. Beyond the

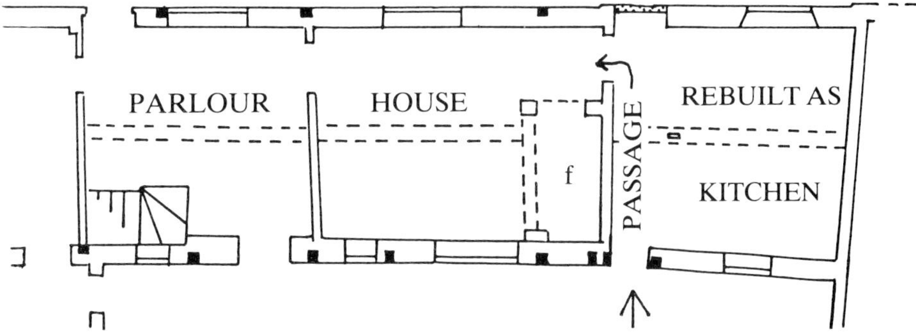

Fig. 2 Plan of the Thatched Cottages, Melbourne, for comparison.

Georgian end, at the beginning of the thatched part, there is a window lighting the stairs. This is where the original front door was, and it led into a passage behind the fireplace, at the end of which you turned west into the houseplace. When this house was built it had no upper storey and so no need for stairs. On the east side of the passage, whatever was originally there was rebuilt in the 18th century, giving what appears to be an independent Georgian house which once had a shopfront to the street. It replaces what we call the 'low end' of the original house, i.e. the part beyond the passage on the other side from the houseplace. At the 'upper end', this time to the west, was the original parlour.

At 56 Potter Street (cover picture) is a small, pretty, timber-framed house with a passage at the eastern end running through to the garden. From the passage you turn west into the houseplace and can see the inglenook backing onto the passage. There is a small inner room beyond. At this house there is no low end on the east side of the passage, but I suspect there may once have been one because the timber frame looks as if it once went on further east. In any case, this is still a hearth-passage house.

At Alvaston, Church Farm *(Fig. 3)* was converted to have a hearth-passage plan in the 17th century. A fireplace and chimney were built in what had been an open hall, leaving room behind it for a passage, at one end of which there is still a door. On the other side of the passage is a narrower low end which has either been rebuilt or newly built in the 17th century to complete the plan. The original parlour remains at the upper end.

It is possible there was once a hearth-passage entry at Old Rectory Farm and Cottage, Weston on Trent. This also had a medieval open hall and has been converted. A hearth-beam shows where the inglenook fireplace was built, and a blocked doorway in the north wall is in the right position to have led into a passage behind the hearth, although that end of the house was later rebuilt and so no passage remains.

One big question about hearth-passage houses is the function of the room beyond the passage at the low end. In every case described above, that end has either been rebuilt or has disappeared altogether, so why did this happen? The replacement rooms built at the low end at Repton and the Thatched Cottages, Melbourne, had west gables and chimneys and may have been kitchens, which would be required once it became no longer acceptable to do the cooking in the houseplace.

Before that, the low end must have had some function that caused it to be unsuitable to turn it into a kitchen without rebuilding, and our guess is that it may have been a cowshed. Most village dwellers in the Middle Ages and well into the 17th century kept a milk cow, and one design of house does include accommodation for the cows and the family under the same roof, with a common entrance. That is the 'Longhouse', a translation of the Welsh name for such houses, which were at one time common in the Principality. There was a hearth-passage entrance in longhouses, giving access to both parts of the building. We cannot be sure that this was the original design of houses in our region, but it does seem likely.

Fig. 3 The western end of Church Farm, Alvaston, to show part of the cruck couple. Photograph: Derby City Museum.

You will have noticed that all these houses have undergone alterations. In most cases the hearth-passage no longer runs right through the house. A little further north in Derbyshire, Alison Uttley was brought up in a house which had a passage running through the kitchen. She wrote: "While I ate my breakfast, the two doors of the kitchen were flung wide open and the wind rushed down and howled through the house, tearing out of the opposite door". Even if the passage was fully divided off from the kitchen, one can see why this design could have become unpopular.

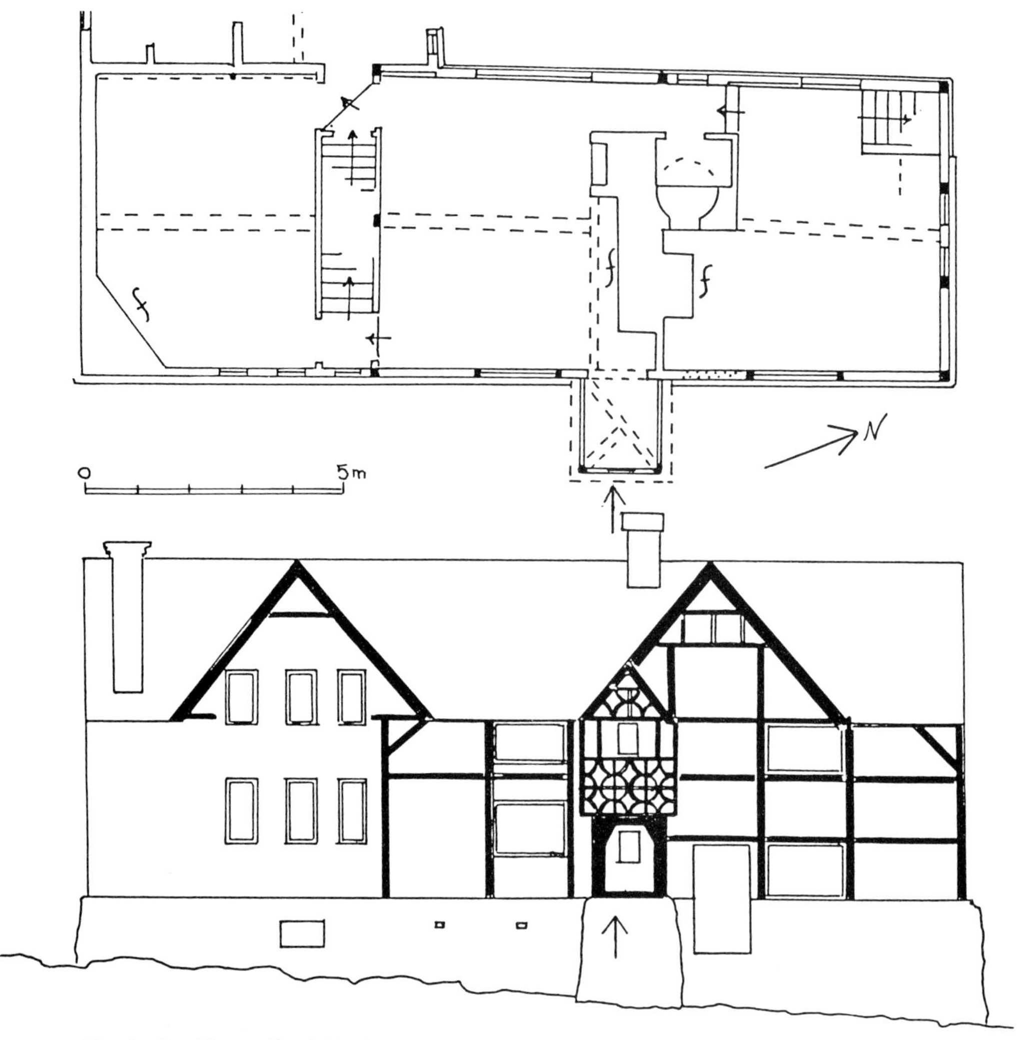

Fig. 4 Key House, Castle Donington. The original entrance was by way of the handsome porch.

LOBBY ENTRANCE HOUSES

The three-cell lobby entrance plan can be seen at Key House, Castle Donington *(Fig. 4)*. Here there was never a passage, but the original entrance was by way of the porch dated 1595 into a tiny lobby in front of the chimneystack. The fireplaces have since been rebuilt and altered, but it is clear that there was originally a pair of back-to-back inglenooks for the houseplace on the south side and the kitchen on the north. On the east side of the stack where there is now a cupboard, the stairs once went up northwards from the houseplace, over the top of the bread oven beside the kitchen hearth. The third room at the south end of the house was the parlour. The Old Talbot Inn at Hilton *(Fig. 5)* was also

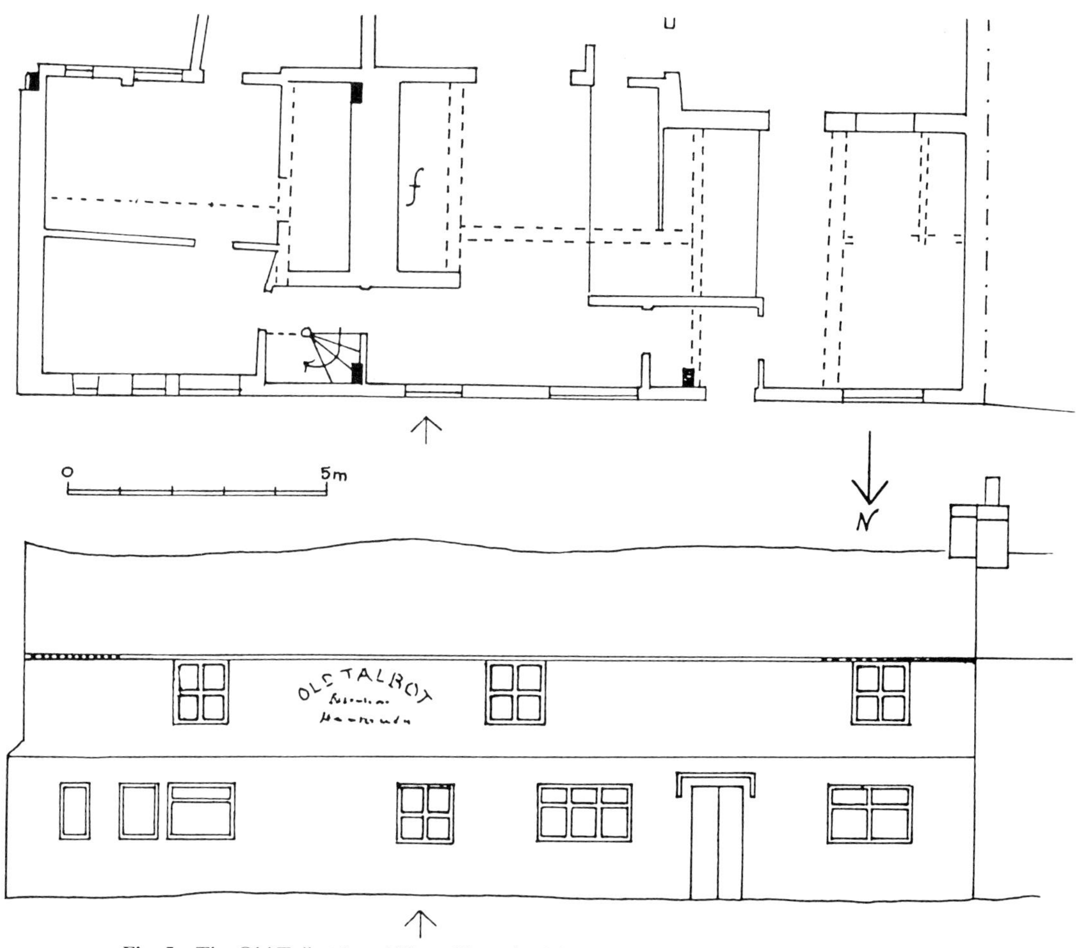

Fig. 5 The Old Talbot Inn, Hilton. There is a big double chimney with the original entrance marked by an arrow.

built to this plan. The original entrance was opposite the double chimney, which served a fireplace for the houseplace on the west side and the kitchen on the east. A narrow stair still goes up beside the former front door. To separate the public from the private rooms, a new doorway was later made between the houseplace and the west parlour, where the bar now is, leaving the kitchen and the upper rooms for the family's use. Similarly at Castle Farm, Melbourne, the original main entrance (where there is now an added-on cloakroom) was opposite a double chimney. The houseplace was on the north side and the kitchen on the south; later the houseplace became the kitchen, using the former parlour at the north end as a buttery, and the original kitchen was turned into a parlour which could be used as a sort of farm office. Another house of this type was found at Aston, dated 1691; there was here a single central stack which had a fire-window in the west wall to light the chimney-corner; the stairs went up on the eastern side of the stack. The parlour at the north end was originally unheated, and at the southern end of the house there was a range of service rooms running back to the east as a wing.

A number of houses of this basic design were two-cell, the most striking being Tudor Lodge at Repton *(Fig. 6)*. The northern room was a kitchen and the southern a parlour - in contrast to the house just described at Aston, this house seems to have had no service rooms at all. On the other hand, it is a three-storey house, the attics being habitable, and in its central chimneystack are flues for five fireplaces: kitchen, parlour, kitchen chamber, parlour (best) chamber and porch chamber. Four of these have beautifully cut stone fireplaces *(Fig. 39)*, the kitchen having a timber hearth-beam. The stairs in this house went up on the far side of the chimney from the entrance, rising towards the north from the parlour. The quality of this house, shown in the porch and the fine fireplaces, suggests that it was built for a gentleman, possibly a younger son or brother of a wealthy landowner.

At Mackworth a small timber-framed house has only one original hearth; the framing makes clear that it served the houseplace and the second ground-floor room was probably a buttery. The present stairs are outside the original frame, but probably went up between the front door and the chimney.

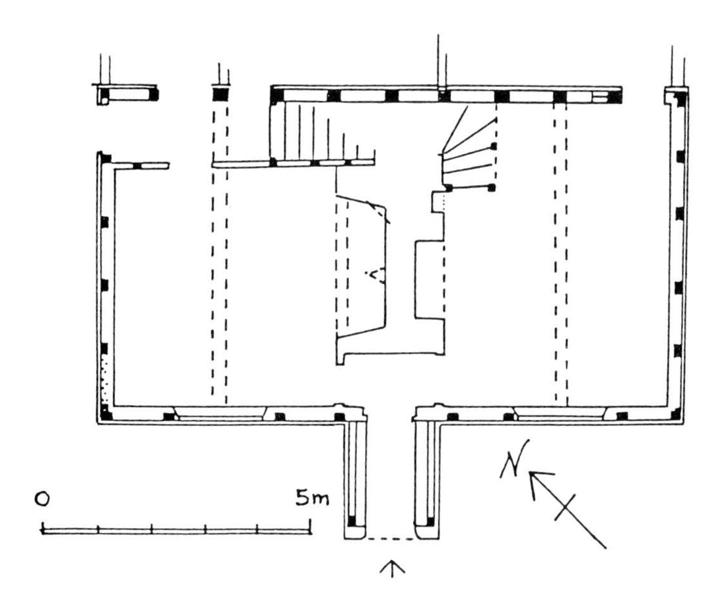

Fig. 6 Tudor Lodge, Repton. The 19th century engraving shows the house as it was then used, as a Village Institute, with a Savings Bank to the left and a Reading Room to the right of the porch.

A house in Trent Lane, Kings Newton *(Fig. 7)* also has a single original hearth with the stairs going up between it and the front door. A second fireplace to heat the parlour was built across the corner in the room behind the stack, and probably replaces an earlier bread oven

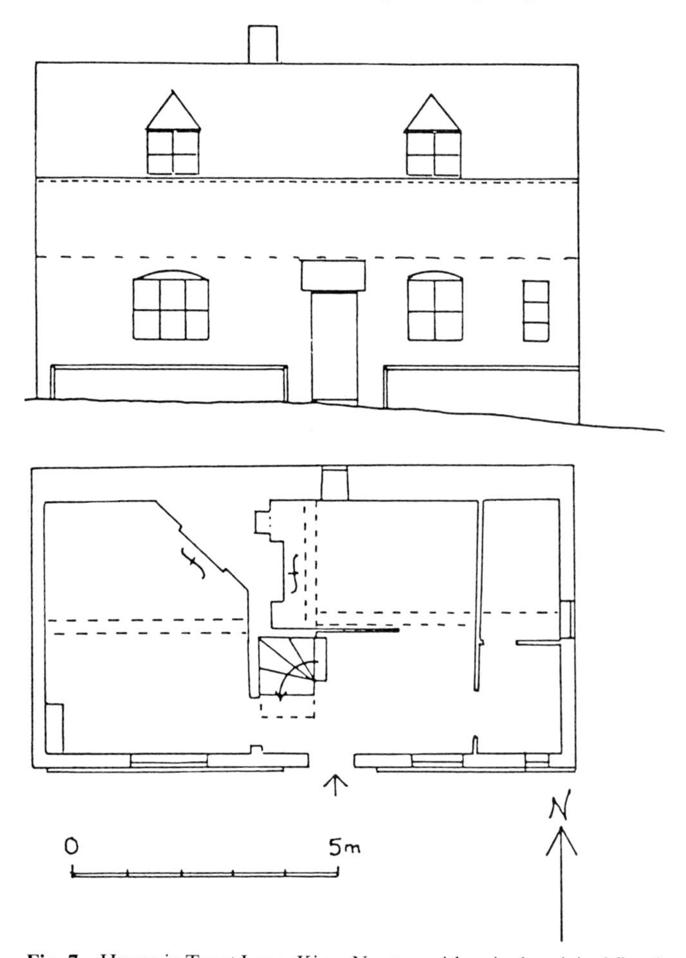

Fig. 7 House in Trent Lane, Kings Newton with a single original fireplace

reached from the houseplace, making use of the existing flue. This house has a thick brick wall remaining from an earlier building, but as it stands was probably built around 1725. Another Kings Newton house, in Jawbone Lane, also had a single stack with stairs going up between it and the front door; the window frames suggest a mid-18th century date.

These plans show how adaptable the central lobby-entrance design was to a wide range of requirements - more or fewer service rooms, a wide or narrow street frontage, and so on.

A different type of two-cell lobby-entrance house is seen at Hatton *(Fig. 8)*. It is a large house, and on the front wall the framing makes clear the superior status of the western end. Right at the end of the front wall the original entrance led into a lobby that must have had a

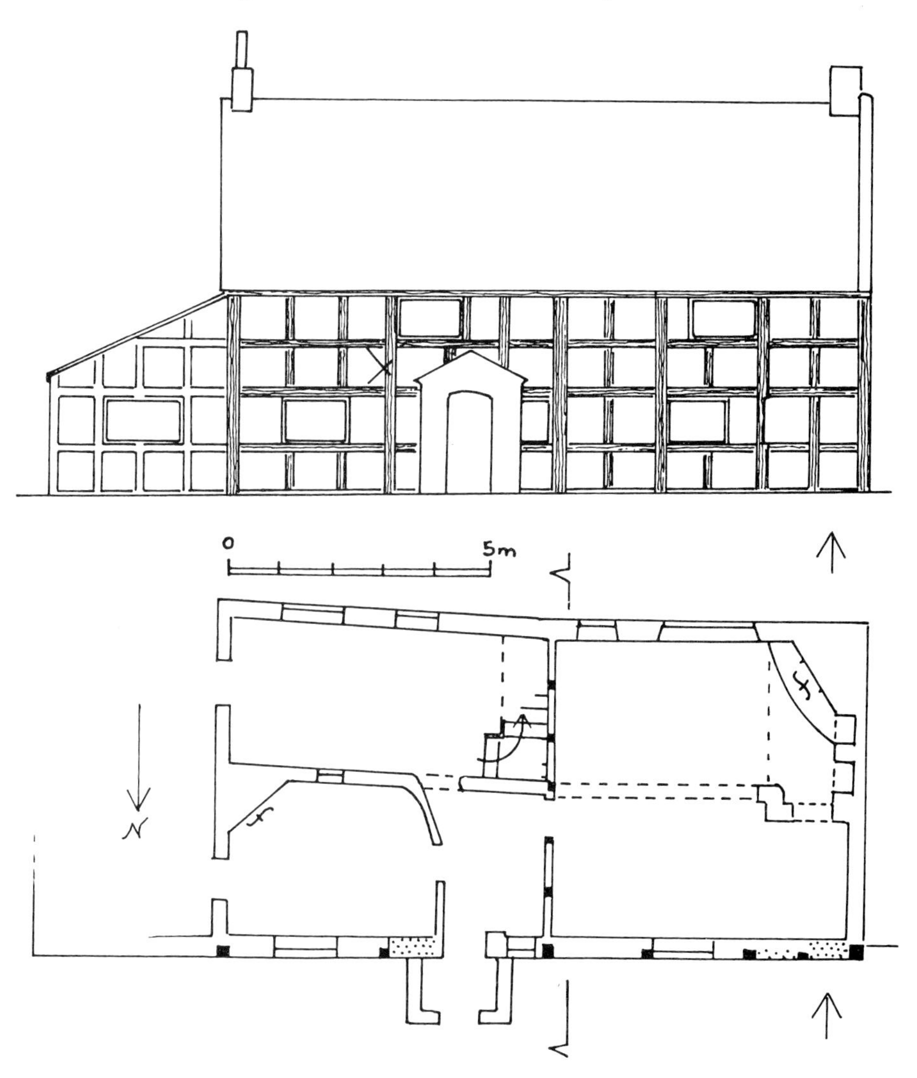

Fig. 8 A house at Hatton which originally had its entrance right at the western end of the front wall.

stair going up against the side of the big inglenook fireplace. The other end of the house was divided lengthways into two service rooms. This is an early 17th century house; an 18th century version at Castle Donington, built of brick, has a similar plan but less generous dimensions. *(Fig. 9)*.

Two two-cell houses we have recorded have central chimneystacks but no lobby entry. At Stone House, Repton, the fireplace heats the houseplace to the east whilst the western room is, and may always have been, a shop, presumably entered by a gable-end doorway in its south wall. At Old Hollow Cottage, Mickleover *(Fig. 10)*, both houseplace and parlour are heated from the central stack, but the entrance was probably in the middle of the houseplace wall.

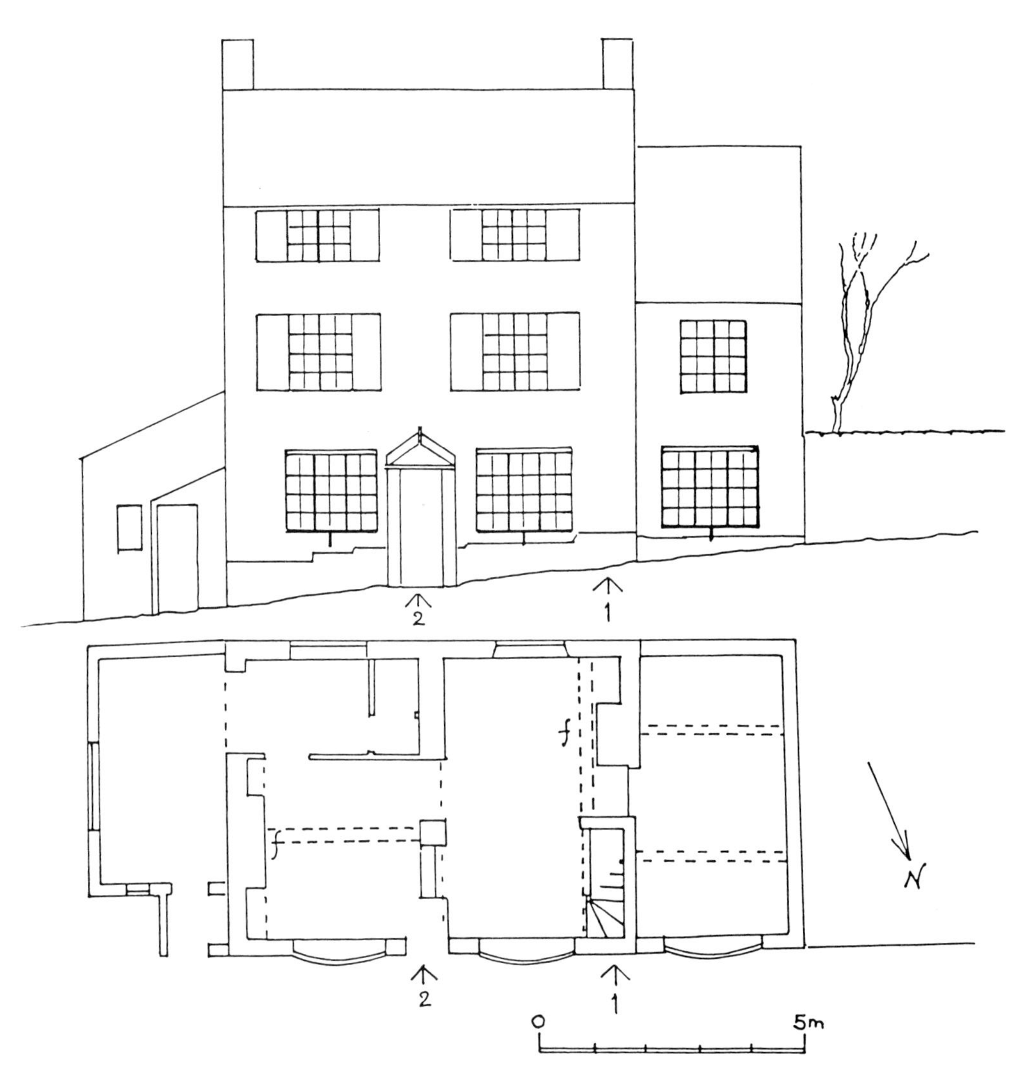

Fig. 9 This house at Castle Donington first had its entrance where the enlarged staricase now is, beyond which there is an addition.

A pair of cottages at Repton had their entrances at opposite ends of the building from the central chimneystack, which both shared. They are now one house, but originally each had an end doorway into a lobby away from the stack, behind which was a small service room. The stairs went up beside the back-to-back hearths, one on each side.

DIRECT ENTRY PLANS

The house plan with two end chimneys and a central doorway opening directly into the houseplace arrives later in this area than elsewhere, apparently following on from plans with other chimney positions adopting direct entry, like Stone House, Repton. In Pinfold Lane, Repton, *(Fig. 11)*, is a cottage built around 1766 with the front door opening straight into the houseplace on the east side, a parlour on the west side and two small back rooms, probably scullery and dairy. The scullery has later been extended to form a separate kitchen, whilst new stairs take up most of the dairy. This house has a chimney at each end of the roof. It is the standard direct entry plan, though in this case, exceptionally, the house is more than one room deep.

Fig. 10 Old Hollow Cottage, Mickleover, a two-cell house with a central double chimney. Photograph: Alwyn Davies.

At Tonge, Church View *(Fig. 11)* has a similar plan that is one room deep though three rooms long. The entrance is into the central living room and there is a kitchen to the west; these two rooms have chimneys at opposite ends, and there is a third room, a parlour, behind the chimney of the houseplace. This house has been altered from an earlier design with a lobby entry beside the kitchen chimney, and that plan is itself a modification of a yet earlier design now lost. Such alterations have often taken place.

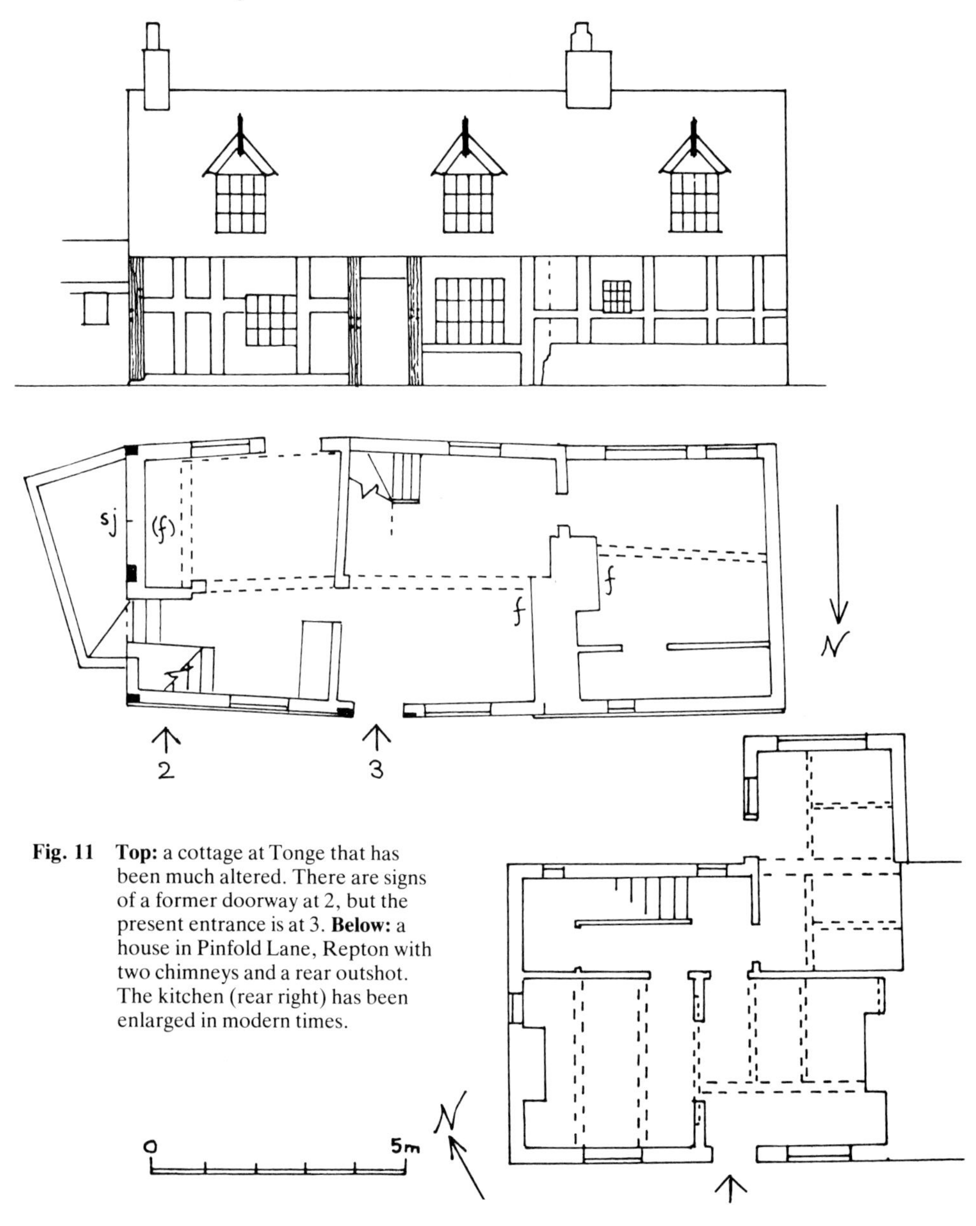

Fig. 11 **Top:** a cottage at Tonge that has been much altered. There are signs of a former doorway at 2, but the present entrance is at 3. **Below:** a house in Pinfold Lane, Repton with two chimneys and a rear outshot. The kitchen (rear right) has been enlarged in modern times.

For example, the 18th century house at Castle Donington *(Fig. 9)* has been altered by rebuilding the stairs to take up all the space into which the original front door opened, and putting a new door centrally. Earlier, a medieval house at Twyford *(Fig. 12)* was converted to a similar plan as its front elevation shows. The door leads left into the houseplace at the western end which has a pantry and scullery divided off from it at the back. On the right (east) is the parlour on the site of the medieval hall but with a ceiling built from a huge beam put in in the 17th century to make an upper floor. The house originally extended further east, where there is now a stable.

Fig. 12 Old Hall Farm, Twyford, now looks like an ordinary two-roomed house with end chimneys, but is actually converted from a medieval house. Photograph: Alwyn Davies.

The direct entry plan produces a neatly balanced appearance with a central (or nearly central) doorway and a chimney at each end, like the houses that children draw. They are very common at a later date; an example is this 19th century cottage at Church Broughton *(Fig. 13)*. However, in parallel with this design developed something rather different, the 'Georgian' house with a central entrance hall. There is an interesting example at Melbourne *(Fig. 14)*, where an earlier house was converted to reflect an 18th century lifestyle, when visitors would no longer step straight into the livingroom but would be received by a servant and shown into the parlour at the south end, which was by this date a superior sittingroom. The front wall was entirely rebuilt with sash windows in a design as symmetrical as possible, though this symmetry has later been spoilt by adding an extra, first-floor window and turning one ground-floor window into a bay. There are also extensive rear additions.

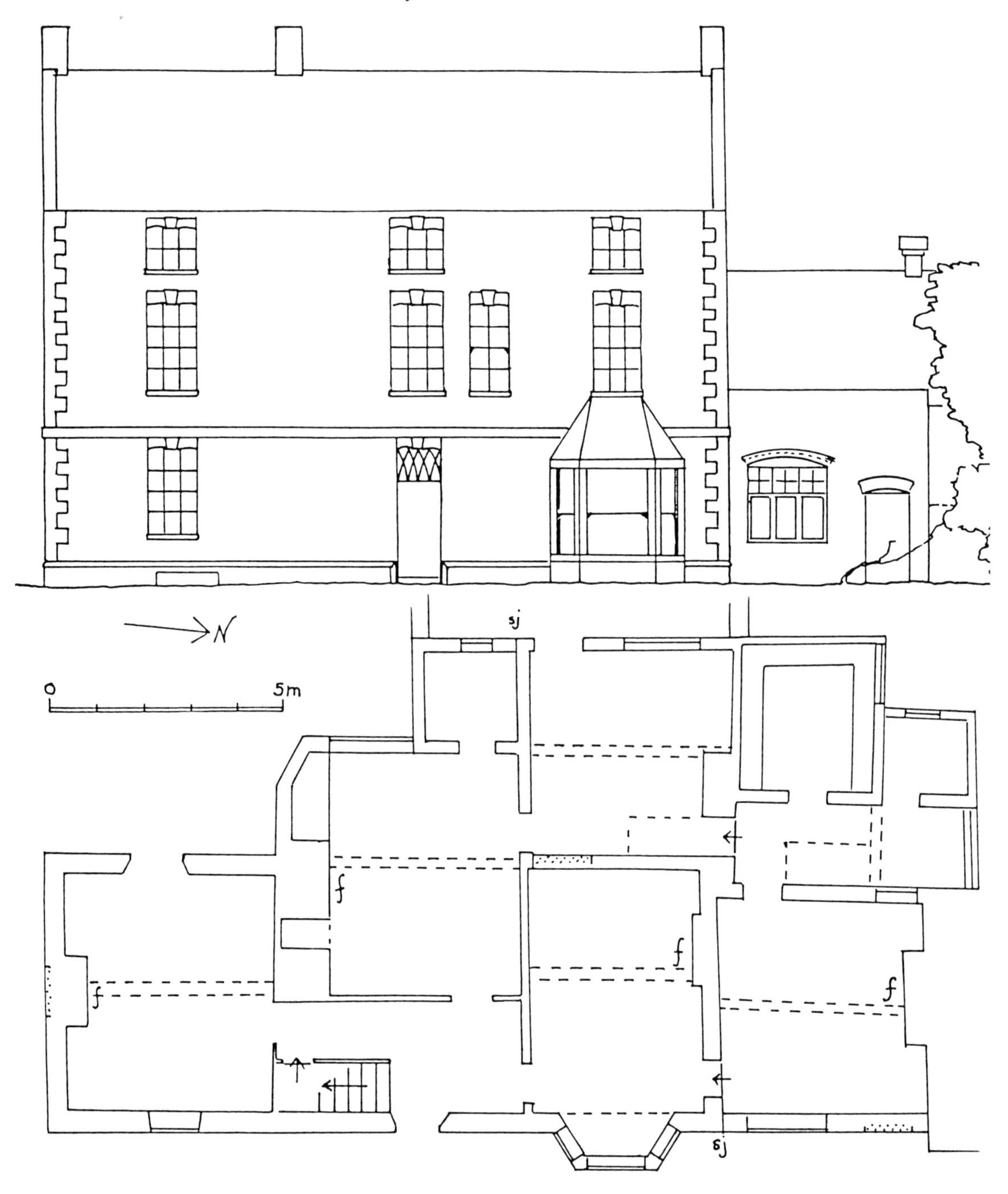

Fig. 14 Close House, Melbourne. From the front this looks a typical Georgian house, but the plan shows that it has been altered from a different design.

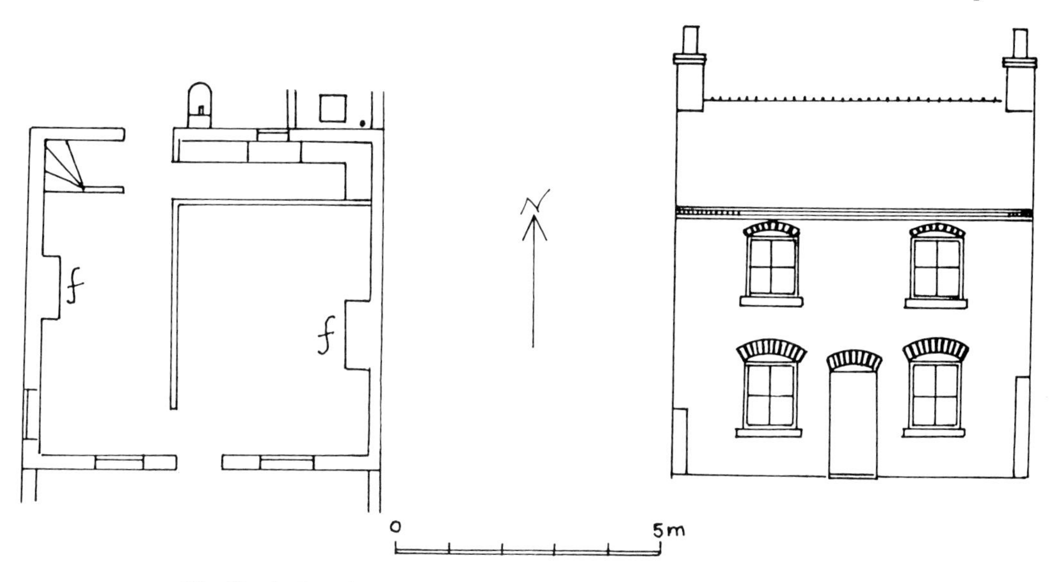

Fig. 13 A charming cottage at Church Broughton, the entrance leading straight into the livingroom.

DOUBLE PILE PLANS

Nearly all the houses we have considered so far have been one room deep from front to back, using tiebeams about 5 to 6 metres long. In the 17th century people began to experiment with more compact plans two rooms deep; but in this region we have only recorded two examples. One is Repton Hall, a very large house that is a conversion of a medieval dwelling, the early part remaining at the back. The other example, Mickleover Old Hall, *(Fig. 15)*, was designed from the start to be a square house of four rooms on plan. It was built in 1648 by Captain Robert Cotchett, a soldier who may have picked up new ideas of house design on his travels. The difficulty of roofing such a wide span is overcome by building two parallel roofs with a central valley; the roofs, however, are linked by a central ridge to produce an H-plan roof (see sketch). This is an exceptional design in this area at this date, though in the next century double-pile houses, like Walnut Farm, Burnaston *(Fig. 15)* built in 1730, became fashionable. The floor area at Burnaston is smaller -78m^2 against 124m^2 at Mickleover - but there are three full storeys instead of two. Both these houses have direct entry into a sittingroom, though many 18th century houses of this design have the Georgian style central entrance-hall. Walnut Farm's appearance is typical of 18th century farmhouses in this area, and many like it can be seen in the fields near Derby.

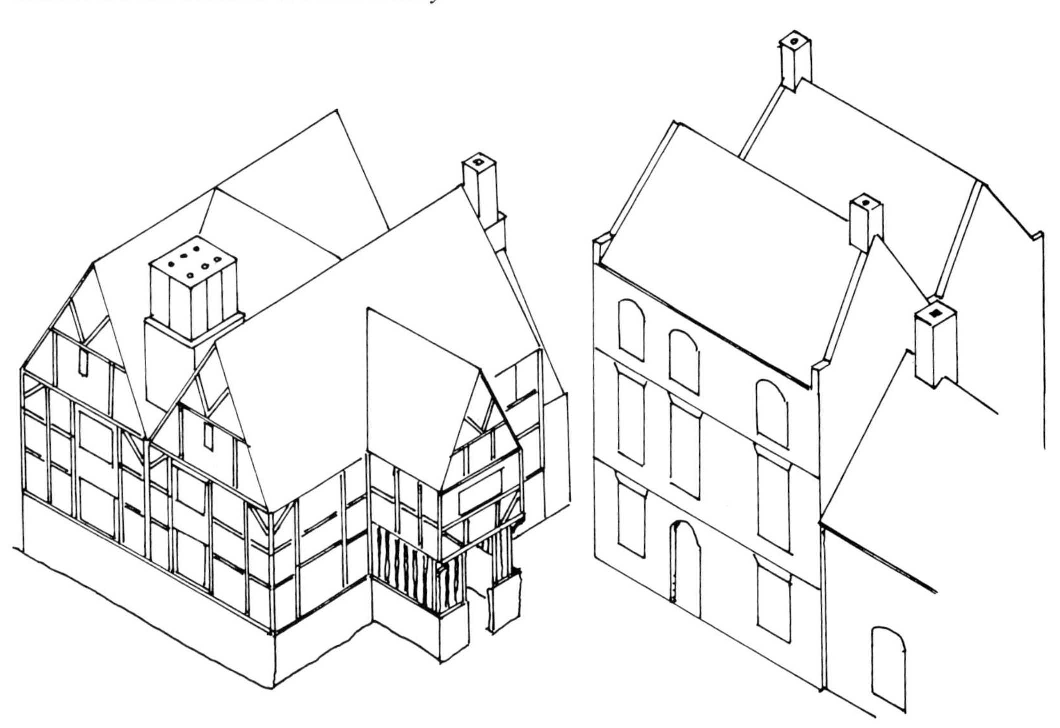

Fig. 15 These two houses have 'double pile' plans but look very different. On the left is Mickleover Old Hall, on the right is Walnut Farm, Burnaston.

Structure

CRUCKS

Some dozen of the earlier houses that we have recorded in this region were built on crucks. Crucks are pairs of long, curving timbers rising from ground level right up to the ridge of the roof. Their advantage is that they transmit the weight of the roof directly to the ground, by-passing the walls which need not be load-bearing. This means you can rebuild the walls without interfering with the roof. Their disadvantage is that upper storey rooms, if there is an upper storey, will be narrow and perhaps obstructed owing to the curve of the crucks which give a steep pitch to the roof. This is probably the reason that this method of construction eventually went out of use.

A good example of cruck building is Church Farm, Alvaston *(Fig. 16)*. It has two surviving cruck couples, the very fine blades measuring as much as 50cm across at their widest point, and rising in regular curves to a ridge seven metres above the ground, which means that the cruck blades themselves are about 7.5 metres long. They are tied into the wall framing at eaves level by spur ties, and the roof is supported on a single pair of massive purlins with windbraces going up to them. The tops of the crucks are concealed by the ceiling but it can be seen in the end wall that there is a ridgepiece running along the ridge of the roof and supported by a saddle at the top of the blades. The common rafters will be pegged on to this ridgepiece. The roof is thatched. The couples, which span some 6m, are widely spaced, being about 7m apart, and this provided a central spacious and high room open to the roof which must have been most impressive when it was built, probably in the first half of the 16th century. However, it now has a 17th century plan with a narrower addition at the western end; the open hall has had a fireplace and chimney built in it and an upper floor has been constructed on a huge ceiling beam with pyramid stops, which crosses the houseplace to carry the joists for the upper floor.

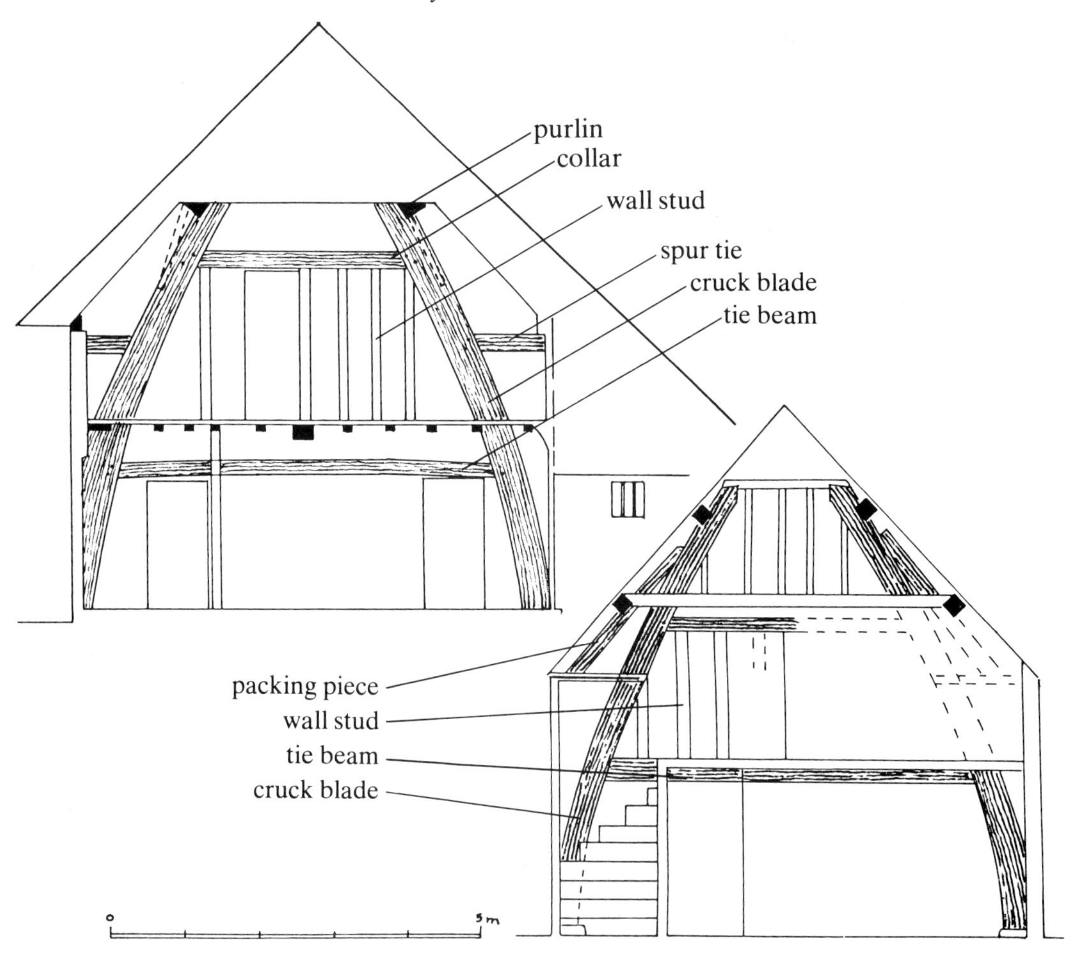

Fig. 16 **Above:** cross section of Church Farm, Alvaston showing the splendid size and quality of the crucks inside. For comparison, The Limes, Allestree on the right has equally impressive crucks hidden inside.

There is a fine pair of crucks in Cornhill, Allestree, with very similar dimensions and the same regular curve, but here most of the house has been rebuilt around this one cruck couple *(Fig. 16)*. There is a massive (43 x 30 cm) tiebeam linking the two cruck blades together at the level of the groundfloor ceiling. On this is built a timber and plaster wall at first floor level, rising up to the level of the collarbeam which is tenoned into the blades just below the level of the present upper-floor ceiling. At the level of the eaves, which is just above that of the tiebeam, there is on each side a short spur tie which links the cruck couple to the top of the outer walls. On these spur ties stand packing pieces which lean against the cruck blades and carry the lower purlins. In the roofspace the upper purlins can be seen, trenched into the back of the blades themselves. These two pairs of purlins which run the whole length of the roof make a framework to carry all the common rafters, which meet in couples at the apex of the roof. Because there are two layers of purlins the rafters are adequately supported without need for a ridgepiece, and the cruck blades do not actually go right up to the ridge. To hold the roof steady against racking there is a pair of windbraces, which in this case happen to be only on the other, east, side of the truss, running up from the cruck blades to the lower purlins. The blades terminate in vertical cuts over 1m apart, and at a later date a piece of wood has been nailed across them to provide the top of a light partition in the roofspace, which was once used as an attic since it now has a plaster floor, although originally the first floor was open to the roof. This apex form is particularly interesting because it is unusual. Known apex forms have been classified by N. W. Alcock in his national Catalogue of cruck buildings, and this is type W; all 59 other W-apexes are found in the area around Oxford where there are some very early cruck buildings. This cruck couple may be 16th century and cannot be included in the same geographical group.

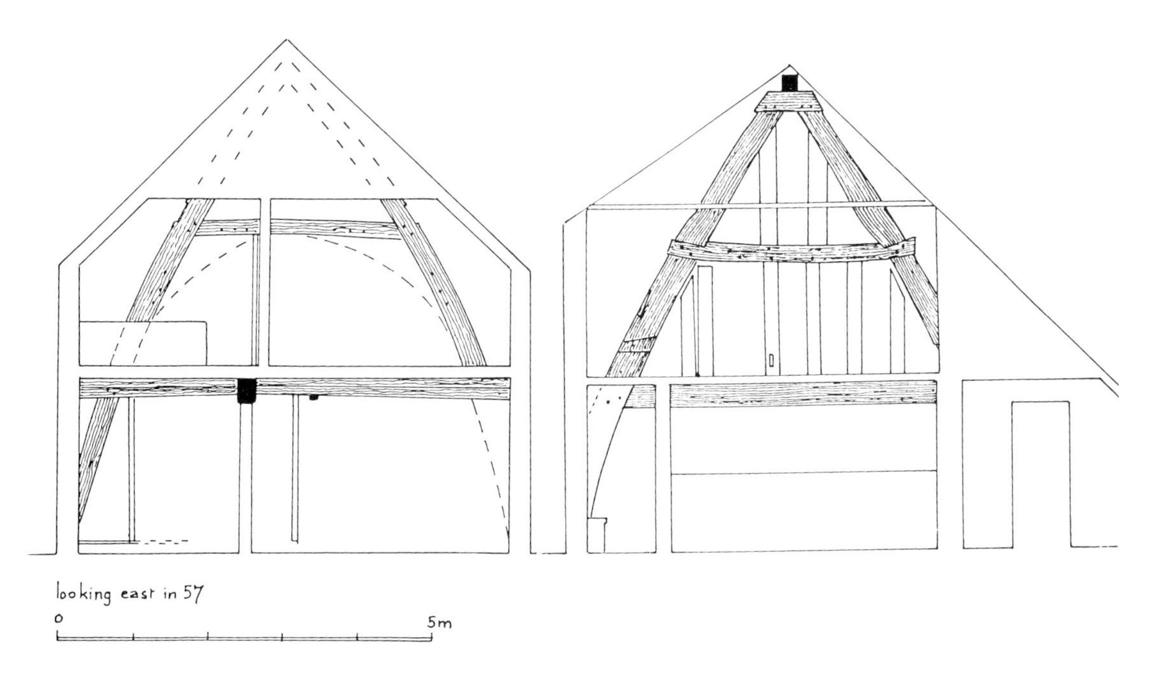

Fig. 17 Still impressive but slightly smaller, **left,** Weston on Trent with fine curved braces, and **right,** Hilton - see also Fig. 5.

A single very fine cruck couple was found at the Old Rectory Farm and Cottage, Weston on Trent *(Fig. 17)*. This has the same regular curve as the crucks already described and is comparable in height and span; additionally it has magnificent curved braces up to the collar, creating a round arch. This shows it was the central truss of a two-bay open hall, but the plan of the original house has been altered over the years and it is not easy to recover the design as built.

At Hilton there is a good set of three cruck couples, where they frame the Old Talbot Inn *(Fig. 17)*. The crucks span 5.5m and rise to a saddle (apex C) 5.8m above the ground on the top of which is the ridgepiece; the cruck blades measure about 36cm wide and 6m long. The couples stand about 6m apart. The tiebeam has sprung away from the cruck and been secured by means of a wooden plate on top of the joint; above this there was a spur tie, its halving now empty, and higher still a halved-on collar. The truss is filled in with original wall studs. There must originally have been one more cruck truss at the western end of the house but it has been engulfed by the later next-door house. Whilst the quality of timber in these crucks is high, they are slightly less regular than those already considered and probably belong to the same early 17th century date as the original plan of the house. At Chellaston can be seen exposed on an outside wall a tall cruck couple completely infilled with close-studded walling built between four horizontal rails tenoned into the blades. The crucks rise 6.5m and span a width of about 5.5m. They are slender, not more than about 20cm wide, but regularly curved. Unfortunately they are all that now remains of a house that has been demolished. The form of the apex is uncertain but may have been A. There are spur ties, and on one side a short packing piece.

The next group of crucks spans a narrower space and is slightly less regular; they are found in a cottage at Tonge and in Bondgate, Castle Donington *(Fig. 18)*, both on the Leicestershire side of the Trent. Those at Castle Donington are a full 7m high and the house itself appears about 9m because it has been cut into a steep hillside. There are three couples with halved collars but where there are packing pieces these rise either from a separate spur tie or from the timber-framed wall where it is not tied to the truss. The purlins have crude windbraces. Two of the couples have crossed apexes (D) and the third, between them, has a short kingpost on top of a saddle; the difference is probably the result of different available lengths of timber. This house is exceptional as the only one we have recorded for which there is a scientifically-determined date derived from tree-rings in the timber, which yielded a date of 1553-4. It is thus probably earlier than the somewhat handsomer cruck house at Hilton, showing that quality relates to economic circumstances as well as to date - though of course we are usually in the dark about both. At Tonge the only surviving couple has a saddle apex (C), a collar halved across the blades as at Hilton, with packing pieces rising from the outer ends of the collar to carry the purlins on their backs. The houses could hardly be more different, the Tonge cottage largely rebuilt at a fairly early date, the big Bondgate house retaining much of its original 16th century plan. A house recorded at Weston on Trent by the Royal Commission on

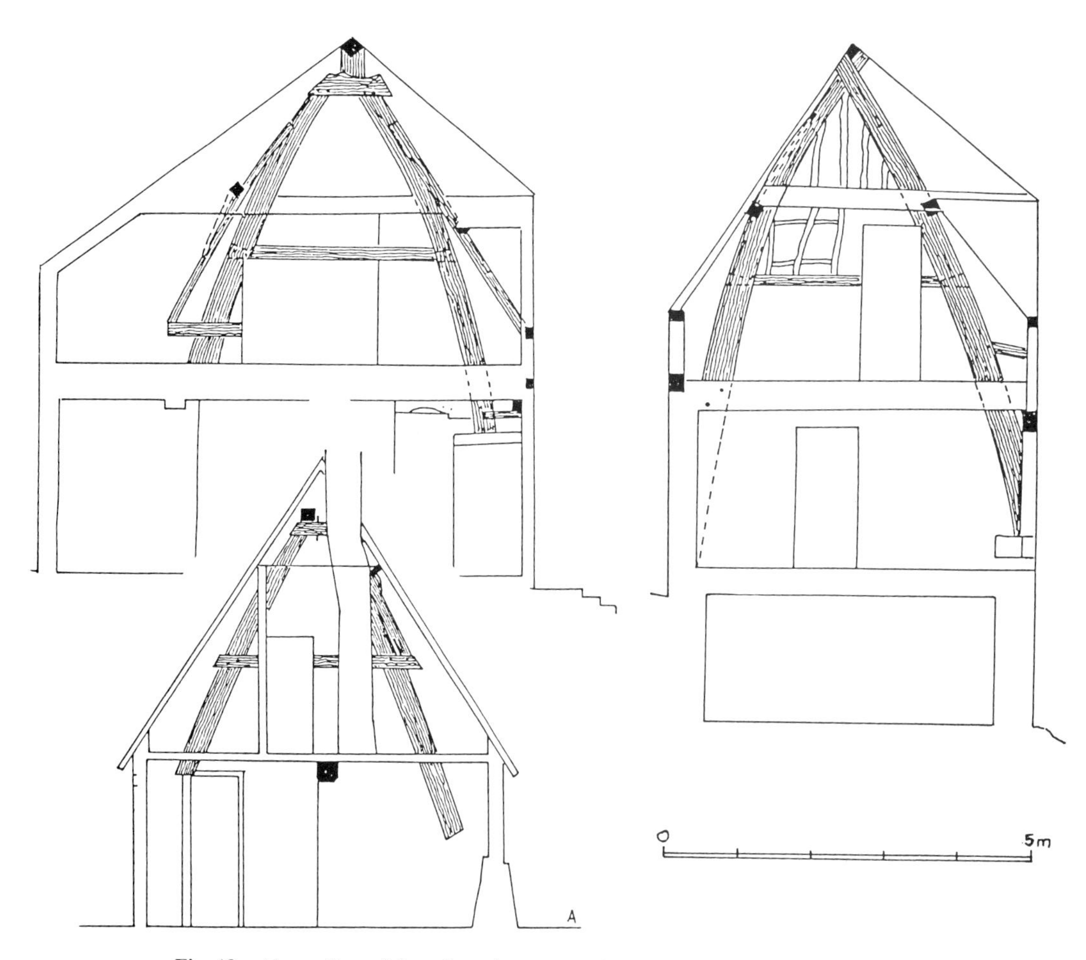

Fig. 18 **Above:** Two of the tall cruck trusses at Castle Donington, dated by dendrochronology to 1553. **Below:** the remains of a cruck truss at Tonge - see also Fig. 11.

Historical Monuments in 1959, after a fire and before demolition, appears from photographs to have had cruck couples of comparable quality with collars and tiebeams, the former with convex braces up to them. The apexes were apparently C, but the saddles had a diagonally-set ridgepiece mounted on them. There were fairly crude, straight windbraces. RCHM dated these crucks to the late 16th century.

The last group of crucks includes four houses, at Melbourne, Kings Newton, Weston and Castle Donington. The last has a single couple of narrow, very irregular timber with the feet cut off so that it is now supported on the upper floor which is 22cm below its tiebeam. This tiebeam and two collars above it are all straight halved across the blades, which do not actually touch at the apex but meet the diagonally-set ridgepiece (apex A). There may once have been windbraces but are none now and all the purlins look like replacements. At Weston there is also a single couple with the lower parts removed; the blades are narrow and irregular and have a tenoned collar with non-matching braces up to it. The apex is concealed and the eaves have been substantially raised so that the purlins have been taken out, leaving no traces. The Old Bakehouse at Kings Newton *(Fig. 19)* has three cruck trusses, one of them exposed to view in the end wall. The blades are irregular and not very wide - 27cm at the most - they span a width of about 5m and the couples are set 5.5m apart. The blades themselves are not much more than 4.5m long, rising to a saddle where the apex is exposed to view, the height to the ridge being about 5 to 6m. From the outside, the house seems to be in two parts because the eaves have been raised along the western end where the ridge is 0.5m higher. At the eastern end there is a half-sunken dairy, so that indoors the room heights are roughly comparable. The couples have spur ties with packing pieces rising from them, originally holding purlins, and there have been halved collars higher up. In Melbourne High Street *(Fig. 19)* a cruck couple is exposed to view in the end wall of no 11-19; inside the house are two more couples, about 3.5 and 4.5m apart. The visible couple has regularly curved blades rising to a crossed apex (D) with a square-set ridge, and with two collars as well as spur ties at the original eaves level. The other two couples, which are those drawn, are much less regular and have saddles with kingposts on them, one apex type F1 and the other, supported by short rafters, F3. They have halved collars and on three of the blades are packing pieces, albeit very slight and poor ones, to carry the purlins.

It can be seen that crucks cover a wide range, from the largest and best carpentered to the most spindly. This method of building has been in use in England since at least the thirteenth century, though it is unlikely that any of the above examples date back so far. All the same, we must remember that because the walls of a cruck house are not load-bearing it is quite possible to rebuild a house around the crucks from an earlier building, leaving them intact. As a general rule, any building technique is introduced at a high social level where the client is

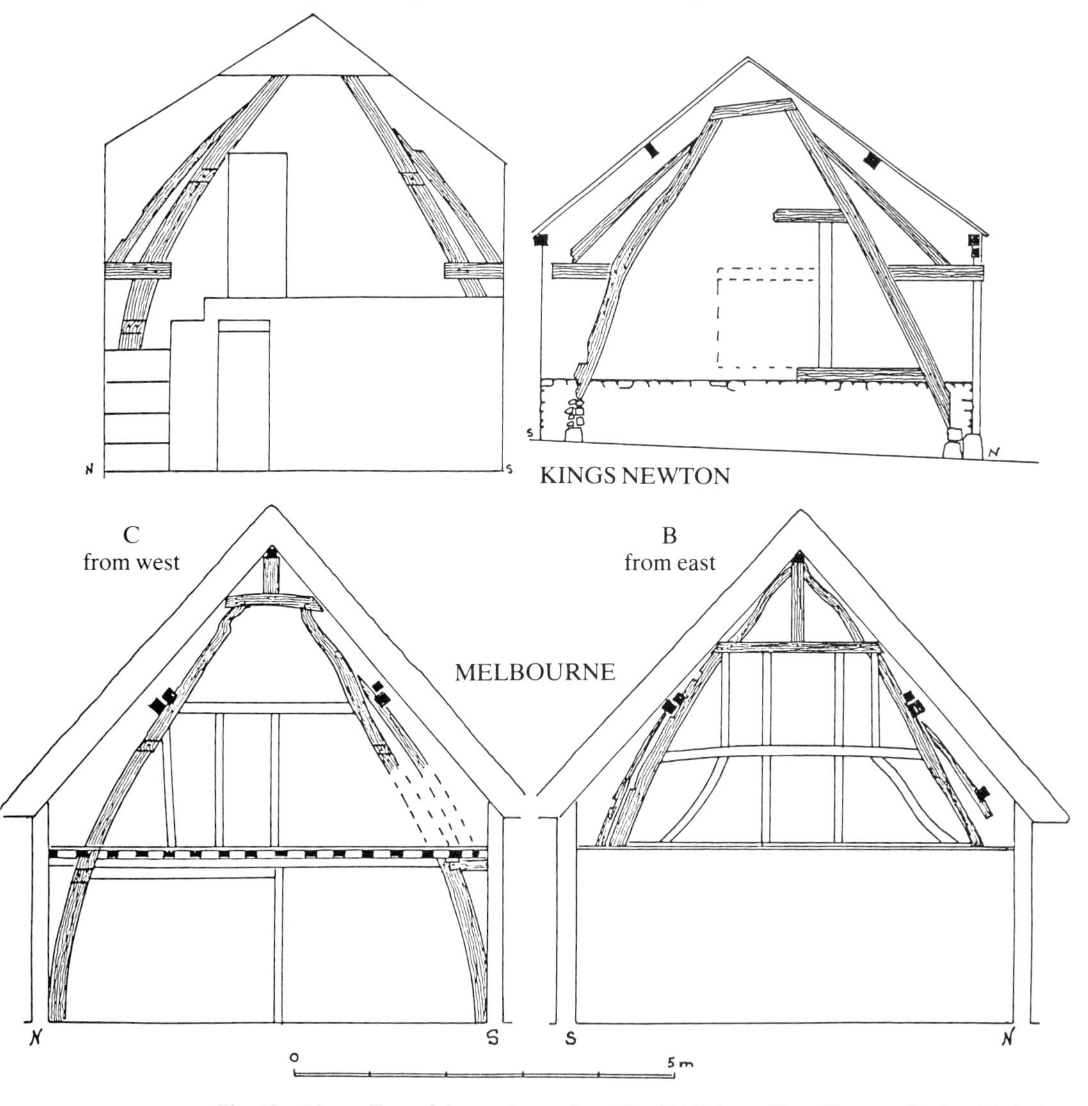

Fig. 19 **Above:** Two of the cruck couples at the Old Bakery, Kings Newton. On the right is the truss visible in the end wall. **Below:** Two of the internal cruck couples at the house in Melbourne High Street - see also Fig. 20.

a man of wealth and position, and is copied later by lesser men until it is in common use even at the lowest social level. This means that early crucks are likely to be of superior quality. At the same time, the availability of timber must be taken into account. Most woodlands were owned by the wealthy classes of society, so good quality timber had to be bought and transported to the site, whereas it might be possible to obtain small amounts of poorer timber from one's own land (e.g. hedgerow trees), provided the landlord permitted. All these factors suggest that the better quality crucks we have described are probably either the earlier ones or were built by the better-off householders, whereas the poorer crucks will have been later and/or have belonged to poorer people. The house at Melbourne is an interesting case. The householder could evidently only afford to buy a single good tree, which would be split to make a matching pair of crucks in the outer gable where people could see it. Inside the house, he made do with cheaper timber, each couple made not by splitting a substantial tree but by using two thin, younger trees that were not straight enough to be worth growing on to full maturity. Such a householder, however, would be far from poor; the homes of the poor in the 16th century are unlikely to have survived at all.

Fig. 20 Cruck house in Melbourne High Street in May 1976 before re-thatching. Photograph by courtesy of Melbourne Civic Society.

ROOF TRUSSES

If a house was not built on crucks, what sort of roof structure would it have? In this region all the 16th century and later houses have principal rafter roofs, that is, the load of the roof was collected by purlins on to principals which transmitted it to the ground by way of the wall-posts. This may sound obvious, but in some regions, notably southern and eastern England, common rafter roofs were used, though here we only find them in early (14th century) houses and those are of a high social level.

An especially interesting roof form has kingposts which carry the ridgepiece. In cruck trusses, if we met a kingpost it was only a short post standing on a high saddle that linked the blades *(Fig. 19)*. In the roof trusses we are now considering, kingposts stand on the tiebeam although they still carry out the same function, to carry the ridgepiece. We have two examples to examine. In Castle Square, Melbourne *(Fig. 21)*, is a house with three kingpost trusses, two of which are drawn. The walls are timber framed and the tiebeams are set on to the top of wallposts which are braced up to the ties with braces usually curved but in one truss straight. From the middle of the tiebeam rises a straight kingpost with a V-shaped notch at the top to take the diagonally-set ridgepiece. Principals rise from the outer ends of the tiebeam to be tenoned into the kingpost well below its head; on the backs of these principals are carried the purlins. The three trusses are similar but not precisely the same, the difference being in the level at which the principals join the kingpost. Another kingpost roof, at Manor Cottage,

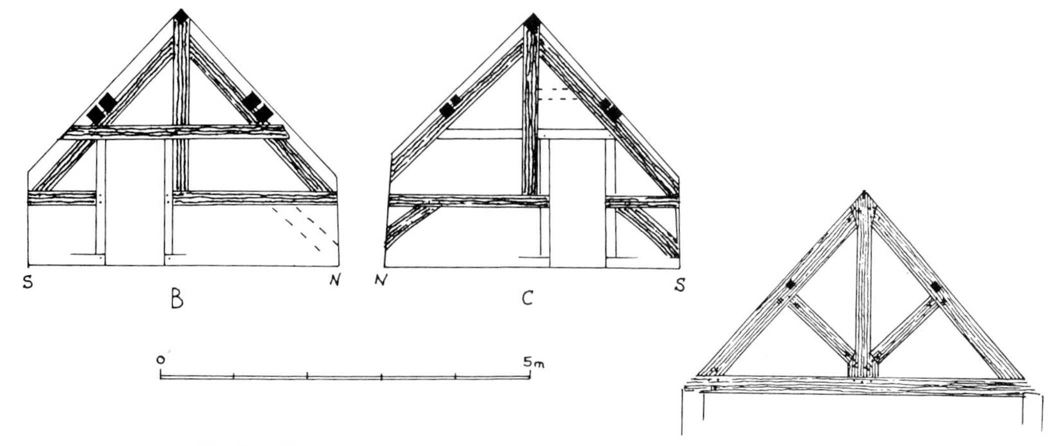

Fig. 21 These roof trusses, drawn to the same scale, span narrower houses. **Left:** two of the trusses at Melbourne, The Thatched Cottages. **Right:** a much later kingpost truss at Breadsall.

Breadsall *(Fig. 21)*, is very different. It is built of good quality sawn oak and all the joints are pegged and marked with neatly chiselled assembly numbers. The tiebeam rests on top of brick walls; in the middle of it rises the kingpost which has a wide, shouldered base and a head swelling out to receive the tenons of the principals right at the top. The ridgepiece is a mere plank, and the purlins are tenoned into the principals on both sides, the so-called 'butt' purlins. From the shoulders at the base of the kingpost rise two struts which are tenoned into the principals just below the purlins. This design of kingpost roof owes much to the carpenters' pattern books and manuals that began to be available in the early 18th century, though the splendid workmanship of this roof is in an earlier carpentry tradition. The widening of the post both top and bottom does not seem to be found before carpenters' pattern books appeared, but once they were introduced, both features became common.

Typologically, roofs with butt purlins are considered to precede those with trenched purlins, but in this region this does not seem to be chronologically so. We have recorded seven roofs with butt purlins and all but one fall into the date bracket 1580-1630 - that one is the roof at Breadsall just described. Trenched purlins (16 cases) and roofs with the purlins laid on the backs of the principals (6 cases) appear about the same time but go on longer. This may simply be because there are more of them. In a large farmhouse at Doveridge in which both forms appear *(Figs. 22 and 23)* it is clear that the roof with trenched purlins was built

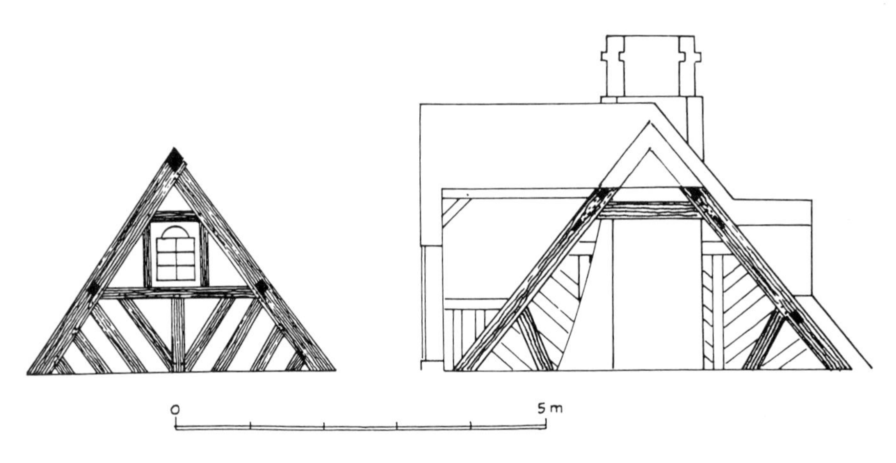

Fig. 22 Roof trusses with butt purlins tenoned into the principal rafters. **Left:** Sudbury Home Farm, Doveridge. **Right:** Hartshorne Manor.

first, probably in the second half of the 16th century, and the butt purlin roof was added on to it later, perhaps about 1600-1620. We have found few dated houses, and the only one with a butt purlin roof is at Hartshorne, 1629 *(Fig. 22)*. Undated examples include Twyford Old Hall *(Fig. 27)*. At Mickleover Old Hall, 1648 *(Fig. 23)* is a trenched purlin roof and other examples that are not dated include Church Broughton Old Hall and the old house in Nuns Street, Derby. Back purlins are found at Castle Donington 1630 and Aston 1691 *(Fig. 24)* where the timbers are of poor quality and most of them re-used. At the Stone House, Repton, which was probably built between about 1700 and 1750, there are no roof trusses at all because the stone cross walls are built up to carry the heavy purlins.

A particularly interesting roof, showing excellent craftsmanship, is seen at Castle Farm, Melbourne *(Fig. 25)*. This roof form is called an upper cruck truss because of the curving blades so reminiscent of true crucks. The blades are tenoned into the upper-floor ceiling beams, and tied back to the wall tops with spur ties. The reason for using upper

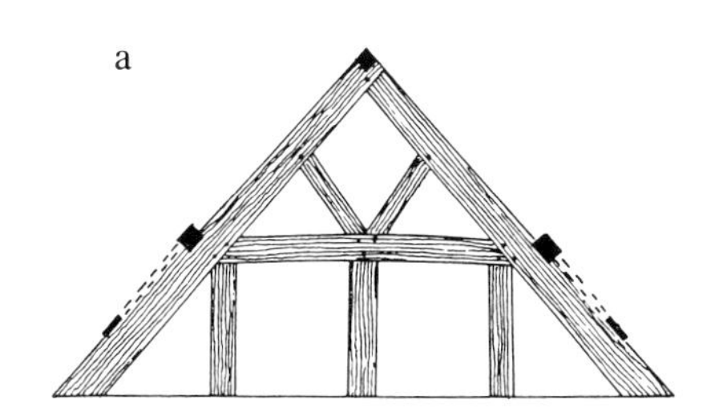

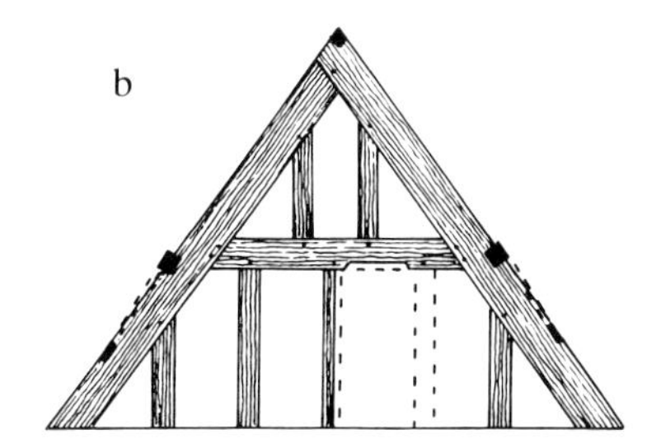

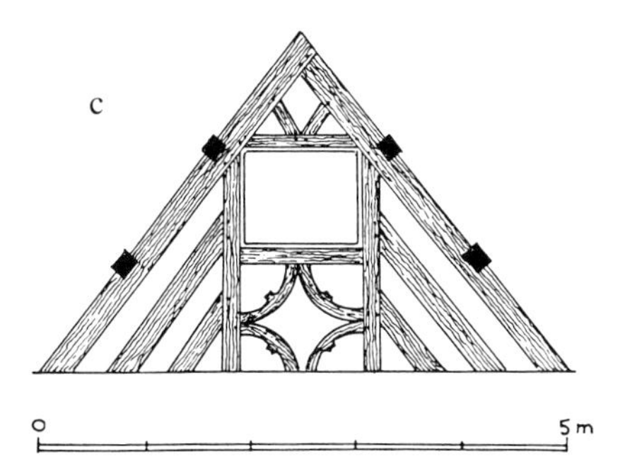

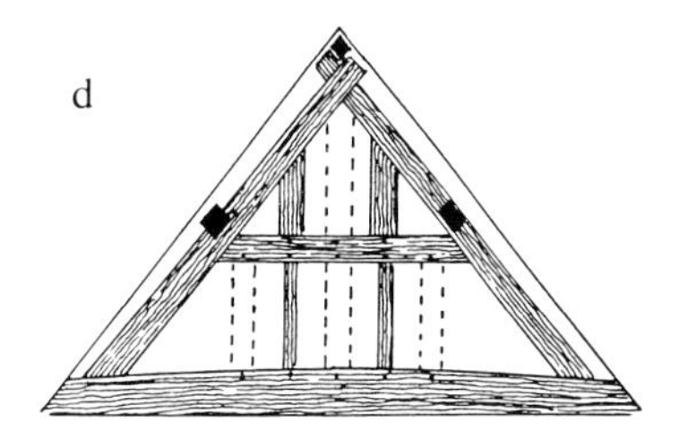

Fig. 23 Roof trusses with the purlins trenched into the backs of the blades.

a: Mickleover Old Hall.
b: Sudbury Home Farm.
c: Church Broughton Old Hall.
d: Nuns Street, Derby.

crucks is clear when you look at the drawing; it is an excellent way of providing more headroom in the attic. At Aston, by contrast, the tiebeam has had to be cut to allow a doorway through from one end of the roof to the other. At Castle Farm the apex is concealed but since there are two pairs of trenched purlins there may well be no need for a ridgepiece. The only other upper cruck truss found is at Derwent Farm, Little Chester, but this is built with re-used timber. Both date from the early 17th century.

A characteristic feature which we have found in eleven principal rafter roofs is the crossed apex, similar to cruck apex D. Almost certainly this design feature is carried over from cruck building, although only two of the cruck roofs we have recorded here have D apexes.

Roof covering was often thatch, and Mount Pleasant, Weston *(Fig. 26)*, still has some of its thatch underneath the present slate roof. There are thatched houses today in Melbourne, Repton and other villages. Tiles have been in use probably for longer than has brick, and here plain tiles continued in fashion until the first Welsh slate (brought in by canal) and later concrete tiles superseded them. Stone slates, though durable, are heavy and require a particularly strong roof frame which, combined with the expense of carriage, has made them too dear for normal use in this region.

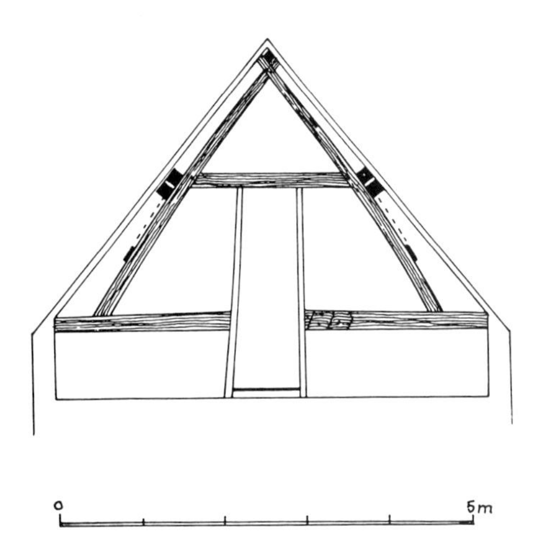

Fig. 24 Purlins laid on the backs of the blades at Aston on Trent, 1691.

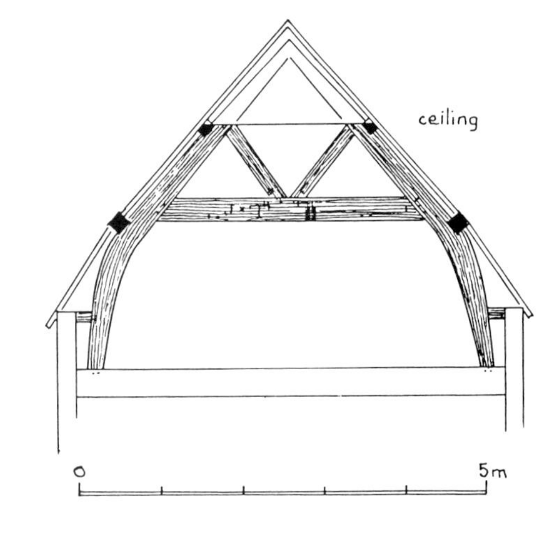

Fig. 25 Upper cruck truss at Castle Farm, Melbourne.

Fig. 26 Inside the roof at this house at Weston on Trent can be seen the original thatch. Photograph: Kenneth Boyce.

WALL FRAMING

When we come to consider wall framing there is a clear developmental sequence, which can be translated into chronological terms fairly closely. In brief, timber walling preceded brick or stone, and of timber walling systems, close studding preceded square panels. This applies to the Trent valley region, though not necessarily throughout the country.

The houses we have recorded with close studding all appear to be earlier than about 1630; at Alvaston the original 16th century frame is close studded, whilst the added 17th century low end is walled in square panels. However, it may be more significant that the houses with close studding are almost all substantial buildings; that is to say, in two cases we have no clue to the original social level but of the remaining ten those that are not manor houses were built by other persons of consequence. Good examples are found at Twyford in two houses, and at Stone House Prebend in Derby *(Figs. 27, 28)*. The studs rise the full height of a storey, in nearly all cases without a middle rail. Close studding can certainly be considered to demonstrate wealth because of the quantity of timber required. In some other areas it has been found that the upper or parlour end of the house is close studded whilst the rest of the building is less expensively walled, but the only case of that kind here is a medieval house at Repton, where the hall has had close studding though the service end has square panels. Similar in social importance to close studding is the use of ornamental panels like those at Key House, Castle Donington (porch) or Old Hall, Church Broughton which also has diagonal studding as is ubiquitous at Hartshorne Manor. (Frontispiece).

The great majority of timber walled houses in our region (26) have what we loosely describe as 'square panel' framing. This usually means that there are full-height studs at fairly wide intervals, the space between them divided into panels by horizontal rails. The panels may be regular in size or variable; where they are regular they are usually fairly small, that is, under 1 metre wide, an exception being the Old Bakery at Kings Newton where they are 1.1 metre square. Some small panel walls have an occasional larger panel to take the window of the main room, but there is a small number of houses with big wall-panels of very variable size, notably two at Castle Donington. The load-bearing posts in these walls are usually distinguished by being braced

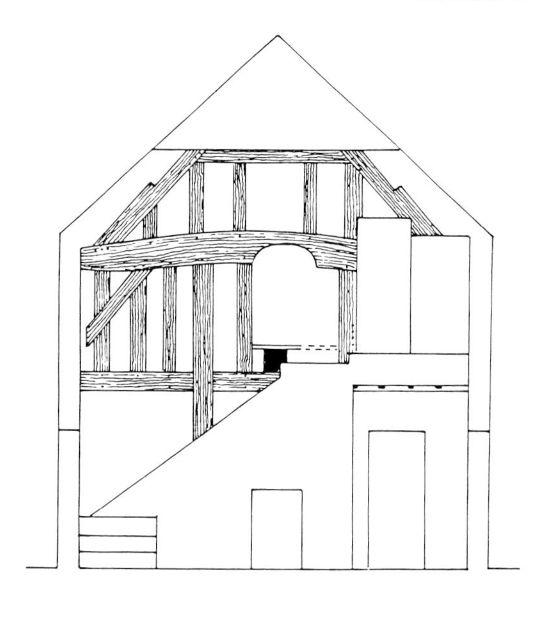

Fig. 27 Close studding at Twyford Old Hall Farm (above) and Twyford Old Hall Cottage (below).

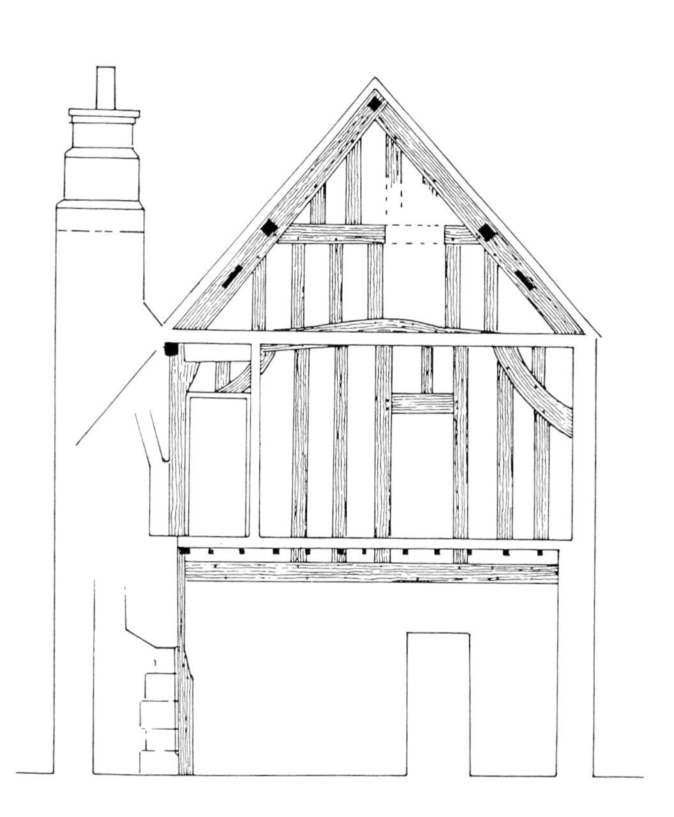

up to the wallplate; early braces are usually curved and later ones straight, as can be seen at the Thatched Cottages, Melbourne *(Fig. 29)*, where the original house with the kingposts has curved braces and the eastern extension straight ones.

Four houses have been recorded with walls four panels high, two to each storey. It is quite common to find walls three panels high, in which case sometimes the ground floor is two panels high, as at 56 Potter Street, Melbourne (cover), leaving one panel wall height for the upper storey which has the roofspace to extend into. Usually there are now dormer windows but they may not always be original. In other cases, as at Mickleover Old Hall *(Fig. 30)* and Key House, there is a high stone plinth with one row of panels to wall the ground floor, whilst the upper storey is a full two panels high. If the walls are only two panels high the house may originally have been single-storey, as at the Thatched

Fig. 28 Close studding at Stone House Prebend, Derby. Photograph: Alwyn Davies.

Cottages, Melbourne and the Thatched House, Repton, or they may have been built as one-and-a-half storeys, the upper storey wholly in the roofspace, as was the case at the White House, Weston before the walls were raised.

In square panel framing a social statement may be made by the number and closeness of the uprights. At Willington *(Fig. 31)* there are three uprights between the posts in the front wall making eight fairly small panels, but only two in the back wall giving six larger panels. At Mackworth the front wall, which is four panels high, has five uprights and 16 panels at the livingroom end, whilst in a similar length of wall at the service end there are only three uprights making eight panels. At Hatton *(Fig. 8)* the front wall has the same number of panels at the high end as at the low end, but at the high end every other upright runs the full height of the wall with rails interrupting the intermediates, whilst at the low end only every third upright is full height.

Fig. 29 Thatched Cottages, Melbourne to show the curved braces (left) of the original house, and straight braces (right) in the added part. Photograph: Alwyn Davies.

One interesting point about wall framing is unfortunately difficult to ascertain. It is whether the posts of the frame rest on continuous timber sillplates, or each post is set on to a padstone and the section of sillplate are tenoned into the sides of the posts *(Fig. 32)*. The former is in the southern and the latter the northern mode, and here in the Midlands we may well be where the two meet. In the four cases where part of the original sillplate remains it is continuous, but we may yet come upon the alternative interrupted sill although it is unfortunately common for the original sillplate to have decayed and been replaced.

In most timber framed houses the panels were filled with wattle and daub, the wattles sprung between the horizontal members with woven withies between them and the whole daubed over and plastered. This cannot normally be seen, but at Mackworth a panel is exposed to view under glass, and is shown in a photograph in Don Farnesworth's book

Fig. 30 Mickleover Old Hall has a high stone plinth and large square panel wall framing with brick nogging. Photograph: Alwyn Davies.

"From Mearca to Clarke-Maxwell" page 70. In a few houses, notably two in Mickleover, the panels are brick nogged. Mickleover Old Hall has bricks laid in stretcher bond measuring 220 x 100 x 45/50mm (which is very narrow); at Old Hollow Cottage they measure 220 x 100mm, but there the bricks have been taken out and relaid in recent times. Occasionally the wall panels may be filled with stone chips; this can be seen at the White Swan, Melbourne, where a full-height square-panel wall is exposed to view on both sides in the public rooms. This is said to be a common infill in the north of Leicestershire, where field stones are also used. However, it is usually impossible to tell how the panels are filled in a normally maintained house.

Fig. 31 Trentside Cottage, Willington. **Above:** rear elevation with widely-spaced studs and large panels; **Below:** front elevation with more posts and smaller panels.

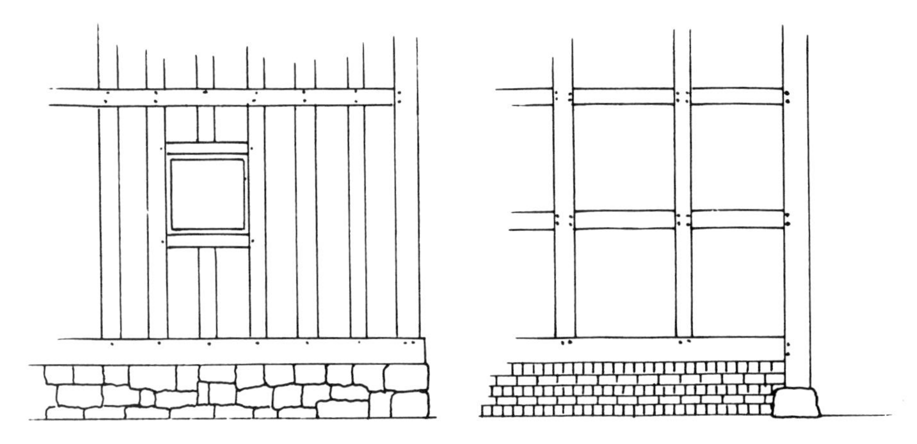

Fig. 32 Sketch to show continuous (left) and interrupted (right) sills. On the left is close studding and a stone plinth, on the right square panel framing and a brick plinth.

BRICK WALLS

The earliest brick building in our region is Repton Hall, where Prior Overton's Tower was built in 1437, but this is of course a very exceptional building, probably with continental influences. The idea of building ordinary houses in brick began at Weston Hall which was built either before 1572 or about 1633. This also is, or should have been, a major building though it was never finished. The brick walls are 70cm thick, laid in strict English bond throughout *(Fig. 33)* and the bricks measure 240 x 115 x 60mm. The Jacobean House in Derby, which seems to be dated 1611, is also in English bond, the bricks measuring 230 x 100 x 55mm, and the earliest 17th century brickwork in the Melbourne Hall outbuildings is in English bond with bricks 230 x 110 x 50mm. English bond, therefore, was the first to come into use.

Castle Farm, Melbourne, is an early 17th century brick house, built between 1604 when the Castle was sold and broken up for its materials, and 1630 when the house appears on a map. It has brick walls with stone quoins, the bricks laid in a form of Monk bond with two stretchers to one header in every course, though the bonding is not perfectly regular. The bricks measure 220 x 100 x 60mm. In Ashbourne Road, Derby, is a 17th century house with bricks measuring 240 x 110 x 55mm, and here the bond is Flemish stretcher, which has two or three courses of stretchers alone to each Flemish course (one header, one stretcher). This house is ornamented with projecting string courses

Fig. 33 The very thick brick walls at Weston Hall are built in English bond brickwork throughout. Photograph: Kenneth Boyce.

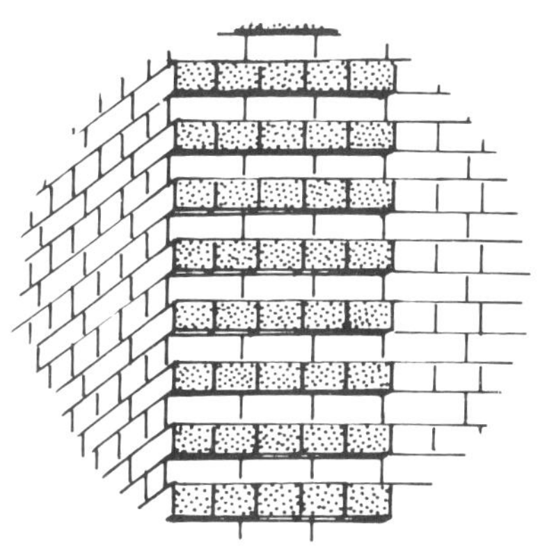

under a heavy coating of plaster on the front wall. Brickwork in three other buildings believed to date from the mid 18th century is in Flemish stretcher bond 3:1 or 4:1, and the bricks there measure 230 x 110 x 60/65/70mm. In each case the bonding is not meticulously adhered to; but it seems that variations on Flemish bond became the normal vernacular bond for this region, rather than variants of English bond. There are very 'loose' bonds with a low proportion of headers to bind the two faces of the wall together; on the fronts of houses with any social pretensions, Flemish bond, with alternating headers and stretchers in every course, became customary, but this was clearly on grounds of appearance rather than strength, and was a national trend. At the same time, there was a tendency for the bricks to become rather thicker as time went on, so that some 19th century bricks were 70, 75 or even as much as 80mm thick.

A few houses in our region are decorated with diaper work with blue (or burnt) headers: this is the pattern found at Sudbury Hall (1671). Close House, Melbourne has diaper patterns on the gable and facing the church, though the Georgian front has been rebuilt. At Aston on Trent a house dated 1691 has diaper work covering the front wall up to

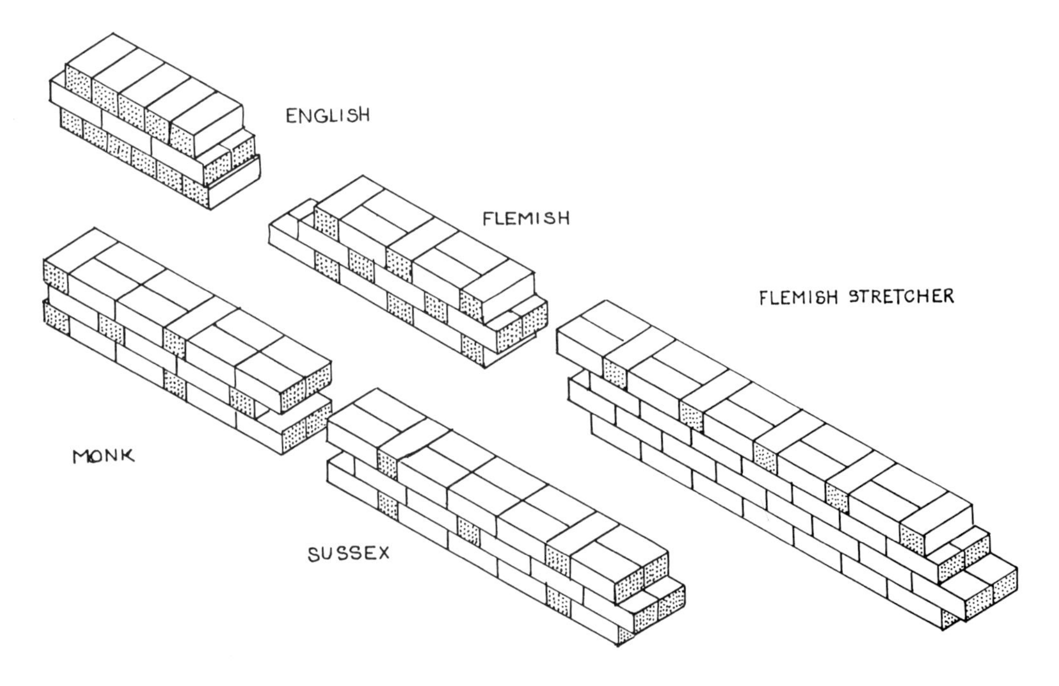

Fig. 34 The kinds of brick bonding most often found in this locality.

two-thirds of its height. The bricks measure 223 x 110 x 55mm and where there is no pattern are laid in Flemish stretcher bond. A band of diaper work ornaments the earliest part of Cliff House, Weston, where there is also a flat string course between the storeys; the bricks there measure 230 x 100 x 55mm. In both these houses there has been a fire window within the inglenook to light the chimney-corner, a feature not very common hereabouts. Diaper work in many parts of England is confined to the 16th century, but in our region as in most of Leicestershire the late 17th century seems to be the time when it was fashionable.

Fig. 35 Traces of diaper brickwork at Cliff House, Weston on Trent. Photograph: Kenneth Boyce.

It is possible that some walling was made of unbaked clay, mud or turf. RCHM believed a house now demolished at Weston on Trent had had mud walls as built, because there were no stud mortices in the soffit of the timber wallplates. This may also have been the case at Mount Pleasant, Weston, and possibly at Melbourne High Street and some other houses where the original wallplates cannot be seen. Such houses do not need to have been low in the social scale, since mud walls give excellent heat insulation and are not damp if properly maintained -indeed, clay is recommended as a walling material in early 19th century pattern books.

Fig. 36 Diaper brickwork at Close House, Melbourne (see also Fig. 14). Photograph Alwyn Davies.

STONE WALLS

Stone is to be found in several places in our region — houses at Castle Donington are built into the rock and quarries are also known at Melbourne where stone for the Castle was obtained, at Repton for the Priory, and at Weston Cliff. Stone House, Repton is said to be built of stone taken from the Priory buildings after the Dissolution, though this cannot be proved. All the stone in the walls is carefully dressed and no instances of carved stones have been recorded. Perhaps more likely is the suggestion that firebacks and chimneys in some of Melbourne's 17th century houses were built with material from the demolished Castle. In spite of Cliff House lying close to the quarry at Weston, the earliest house on the site was probably timber built and then extended in brick before stone was used to rebuild the west walls in the 18th century. But at Limes Farm, Breedon, where there are extensive quarries, an earlier stone house was rebuilt in 18th century brick. However, the use of stone to build plinths for timber-framed houses is widespread. Sometimes only a single course of stone can be seen above ground level, but in other cases the stone plinth rises as high as a metre, as at Mickleover Old Hall *(Fig. 30)*.

Interior features

BEAMS

The interior decoration of these houses, whether they are small manor houses, farmhouses or cottages, is minimal. The ceiling beams are nearly always plain chamfered, with chamfers up to 8cm wide (which is a lot) in the earlier houses, stopped if at all with plain or stepped stops. The only variant is the scroll stop which earlier takes the form of a long "lamb's tongue" but later becomes shorter and tighter *(Fig. 37)*. Exceptional are the few cases of ovolo moulded beams and one with a cyma mould, always run out. None of these features can be closely dated and relate more to the available wealth and a desire to impress; for instance, at Church Broughton Old Hall the parlour beams are ovolo moulded but the chambers above have chamfered beams with lamb's tongue stops, using a cheaper method where it would less often be seen. We have not found here the heavily moulded beams and compartmented ceilings seen in the West Midlands or even Yorkshire in the 16th century.

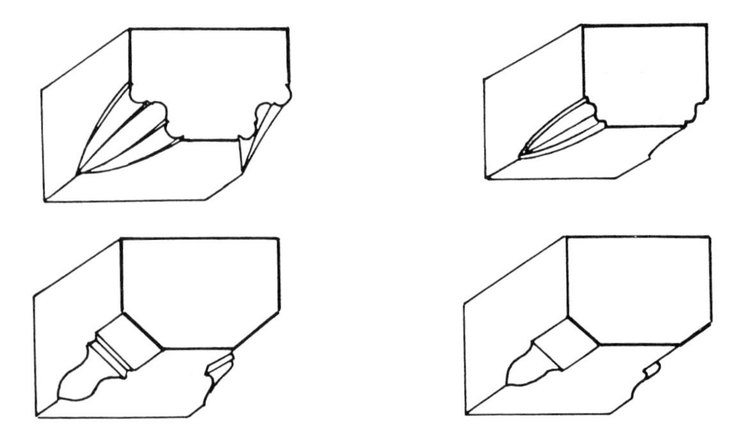

Fig. 37 Moulded beams (above) and chamfered beams with stepped and plain scroll stops (below).

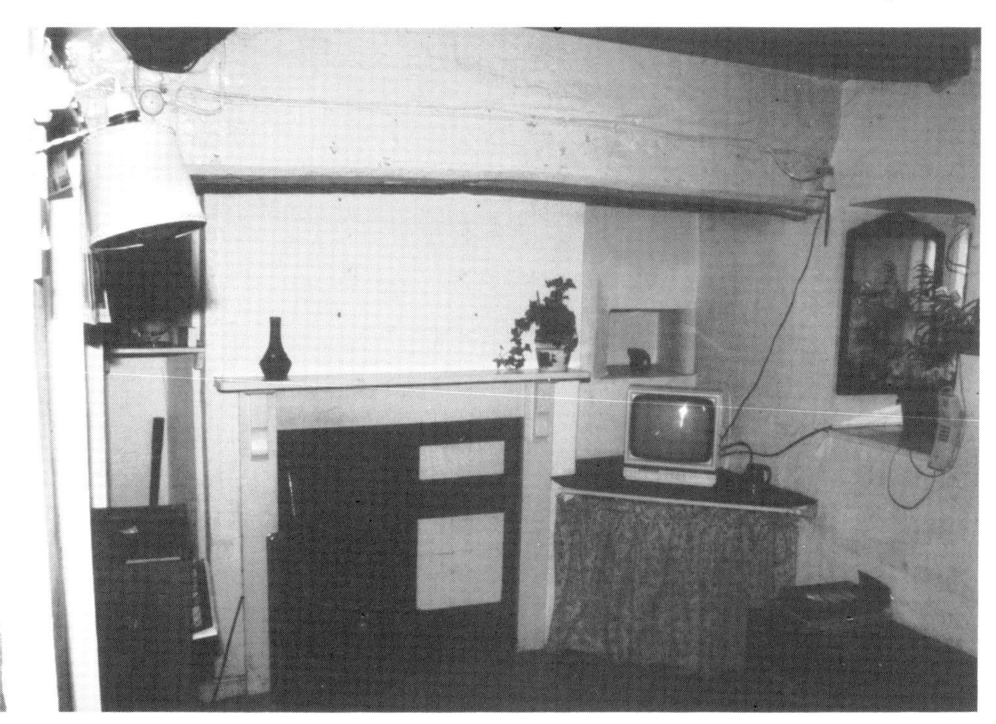

Fig. 38a Fireplace at Trent Lane, Kings Newton. Photograph: Alwyn Davies.

Fig. 38b Newly discovered inglenook fireplace at Castle Farm, Melbourne. Photoghraph: Alwyn Davies.

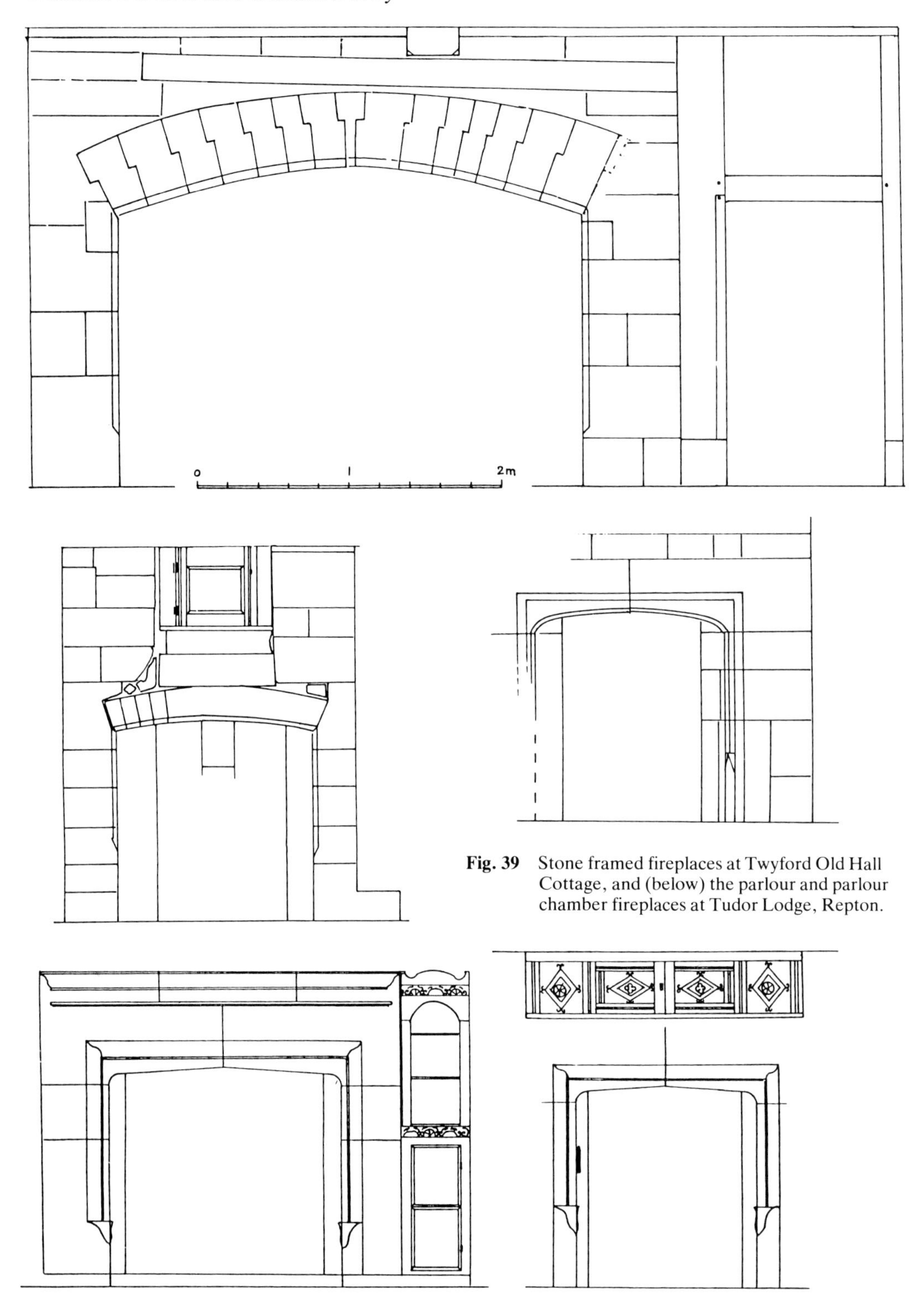

Fig. 39 Stone framed fireplaces at Twyford Old Hall Cottage, and (below) the parlour and parlour chamber fireplaces at Tudor Lodge, Repton.

FIREPLACES

Fireplaces are built as inglenooks under timber bressumers (or hearth-beams), a style lasting well into the 18th century for kitchen hearths even when abandoned in the houseplace *(Fig. 38)*. The inglenook provided plenty of space around the fire for cooking, and gave both light and warmth to anyone sitting inside it. There are, however, only five cases of a fire-window to light the chimney-corner. The position of the hearth is often towards one side of the house up against the outside wall, leaving room for the stairs on its other side, as at the White Swan, Melbourne, though this position is not universal. At Tudor Lodge, Repton and Church Broughton Old Hall the central stacks are not built into the timber frame and leave space for a lobby entrance on one side and a stair on the other. At Twyford Old Hall and Stone House Prebend there are lateral stacks built against the side walls.

A few houses have stone fireplaces, notably Twyford Old Hall and Tudor Lodge, Repton *(Fig. 39)*; these are very handsome with moulded arisses, scroll-stopped at the base. At Mickleover Old Hall there are vase stops, and in the same house is an exceptional brick arch for the kitchen fireplace. In a few of the finer houses, including Haslam's in Irongate, Derby, and Stone House Prebend, there is a carved oak overmantel in the best room.

STAIRS

Few original staircases remain. These must usually have been very simple wooden newel stairs, relying on the chimneystack for support; or sometimes plain straight stairs against an outer wall. A nicely-built 17th century stair remains at Church Broughton, and another at the White Swan, Melbourne, may very well be original. At Repton Hall (1681) is a good open well staircase with turned balusters, and there were also turned and twisted balusters of the end of the 17th century at Mickleover Old Hall though the staircase there has been rebuilt - earlier balusters survive in the attic. Staircases, even in the larger houses which one must consider supra-vernacular, like Calke Abbey and Melbourne Hall, are still built in oak even in the 18th century, which is somewhat surprising since the Trent surely provided a route for the import of mahogany.

Fig. 40 **a:** Stone window frame with hollow moulding at Repton.
b: Moulded stone window frame at Jawbone Lane, Kings Newton.
Photographs: Alwyn Davies.

WINDOWS AND DOORS

In half a dozen houses there are examples of mullioned windows: a hollow-moulded window at Repton and flat-fronted mullions at Jawbone Lane, Kings Newton, both stone *(Fig. 40)*. Wooden mullions were found during restoration at Old Hollow Cottage, Mickleover, and must have been standard in the timber-framed houses. The windows themselves in the 16th century were made to have small panes set in lead cames, and if they opened were casements. These windows might be fixed to the mullions with wire so that they could be taken out and moved to another place if necessary; they were regarded legally as movable fittings, not as part of the house. During the 17th century windows generally became rather larger and the lights were more often fixed. Then around 1690-1700 came two important changes: first, it became possible technically to make rather larger sheets of glass, and secondly the hung sash was invented (in England, in 1670). It was discovered that hung sash windows could be made to the shape of openings that had been designed for the large mullion and transom 'cross' windows fashionable at the end of the 17th century, and in some cases the mullion and transom were cut out and wooden sashes fitted instead. At Repton Hall, built in 1681, many of the cross windows remain but some have been fitted with sashes. However, smaller houses of this date often did not have windows big enough to take the large Georgian sashes. By the 19th century, smaller sash windows like those at the Old Talbot, Hilton, were being made. Another type of window sometimes found is the horizontal sliding sash, often called Yorkshire sashes because they are very common there. These would fit window openings designed for casements, and can be seen, for example, at the back of no. 19 Potter Street, Melbourne.

Similarly, few early doors remain though there are a few simple plank doors inside Limes Farm, Breedon and Church Broughton Old Hall. At Limes Farm and at Weston Hall doors survive in the attics with the legend 'Cheese Room' *(Fig. 41)*, a requirement to avoid paying Window Tax. None of the heavy studded outer doors, common in most parts of the country up to the later 17th century, have yet been recorded here.

Fig. 41 Door of the Cheese Room at Limes Farm, Breedon on the Hill. Photograph: Alwyn Davies.

OTHER FEATURES

Many houses are known to have had panelled interior walls and in a number of them panelling remains, e.g. at Repton Hall. The dating of panelling is made much harder by the frequency and ease with which it was moved. In the 16th and 17th centuries it was considered a movable property and it is quite evident in a number of houses that the panelling now there was not built for the room it is in, e.g. Weston Hall. But in others, like Mickleover Old Hall *(Fig. 42)*, it clearly was designed and built for its present position. Further, 19th century joiners were adept at copying 17th century panelling and it may often be impossible to distinguish between originals and copies. No other form of wall treatment, such as moulded plasterwork or wall paintings, have been recorded, but perhaps the graffiti dating from the Civil War period that were found at Stone House Prebend should be mentioned in passing.

Fig. 42 Panelling at Mickleover Old Hall dated 1655. Photograph Alwyn Davies.

Ground floor surfaces in most houses have been modernised to prevent damp - something our forefathers took for granted and even positively encouraged in the dairy by sinking the floor below the level of the ground outside. Upper floors were either surfaced with broad oaken planks, which even then were costly, or more cheaply built with gypsum plaster laid on reed. This finish is pretty well universal in attics. Gypsum is found locally, is easier to process than lime plaster, and gives a durable surface which has often lasted better than boards. It is also thought to be proof against vermin, such as rats. It is difficult to know how old these gypsum floors are, but it is probably safe to say they are usually as old as the structure of the house in which they are found.

Fig. 42a Graffito at Stone House Prebend.

Post-medieval Houses in the Trent Valley

Post-medieval houses in the Trent Valley region close to Derby were preferentially built of timber, probably with thatched roofs. They were not remarkable for size or opulence though most of the larger houses, which were usually manor houses or of similar social level, have one or two decorative features worth noting. All the same, the average house was well built and has lasted well, adapting to changing times.

Earlier passage plans gave way to those with lobby entrances, and three-cell or longer houses to those with smaller and more compact plans. The double-pile house at Mickleover Old Hall was innovative in its day. Cruck houses gave way to storeyed houses with principal rafter roofs and butt or trenched purlins. Close studded walls are found in superior and rather earlier houses, whilst the majority have square panel framing.

Timber framing gave way to brick in the 17th century, and in brick houses the preference was for bonds based on Flemish rather than English bond. Diaper brickwork flourished here a century later than in other parts of England. Although stone was available, it was not freely used in this region at this time. The general scarcity of decorative features adds to the difficulty of dating our post-medieval vernacular houses. It has been found that most of them have been altered not once but many times, and sorting out the history of such houses, with the various changes that have taken place, is a fascinating study, and one that the Derby Buildings Record is continuing. The houses form a vital part of our national built heritage, and well deserve the trouble their owners take to pass them on to the next generation unspoilt, with their essential character intact.

Index

The index includes a Gazetteer of the buildings mentioned in this study. DBR refers to the Derby Buildings Record and is followed by the building's index number. Reports are filed in the City Museum and Art Gallery, Department of Antiquities, where they may be consulted on application to the Curator. RCHM refers to the Royal Commission on Historical Monuments (England). None of the buildings may be visited without the prior consent of the owners.

Allestree, The Limes, Cornhill, DBR 20. Cruck house with some internal timber framing. Fig. 16, p. 24

Alvaston, Church Farm RHCM and DBR 15. Cruck house with timber walls. Figs. 3, 16, p. 8, 23, 36

apex, p. 25

assembly numbers, p. 32

Aston on Trent, 16 The Green, RHCM and DBR 50. Brick house with diapered front wall, big service end, 1691. Fig. 24, p. 12, 33, 34, 44

attic, p. 12, 25, 34, 51, 56

blade (principal roof-carrying member), p. 23

brace, p. 36

Breadsall, Manor Cottage, DBR 53. Small brick house with kingpost roof. Fig. 21, p. 32

Breedon on the Hill, Church View, Tonge, DBR 5. One cruck truss remaining from earlier building; timber framed. Figs. 11, 18, p. 18, 26

Breedon on the Hill, Limes Farm, DBR 39. Brick built farmhouse with extensive dairy accomodation. Fig. 41, p. 47, 53

bressumer — hearth-beam, p. 51

brick, p. 5, 32, 36, 42

brick arch, p. 51

brick bonds Fig. 34

Burnaston, Walnut Farm, RHCM. Brick-built double pile farmhouse dated 1730 in two places. Fig. 15, p. 21

buttery, p. 12

Calke Abbey, p. 51

cames, lead, p. 53

carving, p. 51

Castle Donington, 31 Bondgate, DBR 23. Cruck house that has been tree-ring dated to 1553/4. Fig. 18, p. 26, 36, 47

Castle Donington, 1 Apiary Gate, DBR 24. Cruck house with brick and stone walls, now reduced in size, p. 26

Castle Donington, Key House, DBR 49. Large timber-framed house with porch dated 1595 and four later dates. Fig. 4, p. 11, 33, 36, 38

Castle Donington, 33 Bondgate, DBR 55. Two-cell brick house with the original entrance beside the stairs. Fig. 9, p. 15, 19
ceiling beam Fig. 37, p. 19, 23, 33, 48
chamfer, p. 48
chamfer stop Fig. 37, p. 48
cheese room Fig. 41, p. 53
Church Broughton, cottage, DBR 26. Nineteenth centure brick cottage entered straight into livingroom. Fig. 13, p. 19
Church Broughton, Old Hall, DBR 60. Timber-framed house encased in brick, with parlour cross-wing. Fig. 23, p. 33, 36, 48, 51, 53
clay, p. 46,
close studding Fig. 28, p. 26, 36
collar beam Fig. 16, p. 24
common rafters (spars), p. 23
cooking, p. 8, 51
cowshed, p. 9
cross windows, p. 53
cruck, p. i, 23
cyma moulding, p. 48
dairy, p. 17, 28, 56
Derby, 22 Irongate, DBR 6. Sixteenth century timber-framed and jettied house and shops, p. 51
Derby, Corner Pin, Chellaston, DBR 10. One cruck truss on the Inn's end wall remains from demolished cottage, p. 26
Derby, 4a Ashbourne Road, DBR 26. Brick house and shop with large central chimney, p. 42
Derby, Stone House Prebend, DBR 57. Large house with two large stone chimneys and internal timberwork. Fig. 28, p. 36, 51, 55
Derby, Derwent Farm, DBR 61. Handsome brick house with string course looped up over the windows, p. 34
Derby, Nuns Street, DBR 68. Timber-framed and brick house with missing north wing. Fig. 23, p. 33
Derby, Jacobean House in Wardwick, p. 42
Derby Buildings Record, p. i, 57
diaper brickwork Fig. 35, 36, p. 44
direct entry, p. 6, 17
door, p. 53
doublepile Fig. 15, p. 21
Doveridge, Sudbury Home Farm, DBR 1. Timber-framed medieval house with additions in 16th and 17th centuries. Fig. 22, 23, p. 33
Enclosure Awards, p. 5
English Bond Fig. 33, p. 42
entrance hall, p. 6, 19

farm buildings, p. 5
Farnesworth, Don (author), p. 40
fire window, p. 12, 45, 51
fireplace, p. 12, 51
Flemish bond Fig. 24, p. 44
Flemish stretcher bond Fig. 24, p. 42
gable doorway, p. 16
gentleman, p. 12
graffiti, p. 55
gypsum, see plaster
Hartshorne Manor, DBR 38. Ornamental timber-framed house with extensive dairy accomodation, 1629. Fig. 22, p. 33, 36
Hatton, 39 Uttoxeter Road, DBR 11. Two-cell timber-framed house with end lobby entry. Fig. 8, p. 15, 39
header, p. 44
hearth beam, p. 7, 12
hearth passage, p. 6
Hilton, Old Talbot Inn. DBR 2. Cruck built house of three cells with outshot. Figs. 5, 17, p. 11, 26, 53
hollow moulding, p. 53
houseplace, also see livingrooms, p. 8, 12, 51
hung sash, p. 53
inglenook, p. 7, 45, 51
joist, p. 23
kingpost Fig. 21, p. 31, 38
kitchen, p. 8, 51
lateral stack, p. 51
Leicestershire, p. i, 26, 41, 45
livingroom, p. 7
lobby entry, p. 6, 11, 51
longhouse, p. 9
low end, p. 8
Mackworth, Thatched Cottage, DBR 48. Timber-framed house of two cells with central chimney, p. 12, 39, 40
manor house, p. 36
Melbourne Castle, p. 47
Melbourne Hall, p. 42, 51
Melbourne, 56 Kings Newton, DBR 21. Cruck house with timber walls, sunken dairy. Fig. 19, p. 28, 36
Melbourne, 11-19 High Street, DBR 22. Cruck house with low end rebuilt as Georgian shop. Fig. 19, 20, p. 7, 28, 46
Melbourne, Castle Farm, DBR 32. Brick farmhouse with stone quoins built between 1603 and 1630. Fig. 25, p. 12, 33, 42